Kaleidoscope Colours of Life

A Living Series - Book 3

notionpress.com

Kaleidoscope
Colours of Life

A Living Series - Book 3

Inderjit Kaur

notionpress.com

Notion Press

Old No. 38, New No. 6

McNichols Road, Chetpet

Chennai - 600 031

First Published by Notion Press 2016

ISBN 978-93-5206-708-4

Dedication

This book is dedicated to:

My ***late Father****, Shri Jaswant Singh Hira*

At times it was difficult to cope with the things in your absence. But because you had seeded the thought in me of believing in oneself and that the power of will and desire is so strong that it can change all the difficult times into a phase that go by peacefully. I now see the meaning of my life and its perfection in every moment. I love you, Dad... And my **Mother** *Harbhajan Kaur Hira* whose Positive approach to life in spite of struggles that she faced fighting cancer is an inspiration for me. Her willpower to face life has made me more determined to face mine.

THOUGHT

"I have seen many storms in my life. Most storms have caught me by surprise, so I had to learn very quickly to look further and understand that I am not capable of controlling the weather, to exercise the art of patience and to respect the fury of nature."

– Paulo Coelho

Contents

Foreword *xi*
Author's Note *xiii*
Introduction *xv*

Part A: Rainbow

1. The Spiritual Violet 3
2. Wisdom Inked Indigo 9
3. Confident Blue 13
4. The Peace Maker Green 18
5. The Optimistic Yellow 27
6. The Compassionate Orange 33
7. The Courageous Red 42

Part B: Contrast and Hues

8. Accentuate Your Positive Outlook 49
9. Act When You Are Stuck 55
10. Appointment with Future 59
11. At the Right Time 63
12. Be a Stand Out- Craft your skills 67
13. Being Committed 71
14. Being Responsible 75
15. Blissful State-Mind, Body & Soul 78
16. Coalesced with Potentials Yet Flooded with Fears 81
17. Craft Your Strength-Be You 87
18. Darkness Will Fade Away 90
19. Dream for Excellence 94

Contents

20.	Expand Your Vision	97
21.	Gratitude Is a Celebration of Happiness	100
22.	Great Influences	102
23.	Keep Walking	106
24.	Life – a Beautiful Collage	110
25.	Life a Beautiful Challenge	115
26.	Life – a Series of Choices	118
27.	Mark Your Presence	123
28.	Master Your Path in Simplicity	126
29.	No Storms Are Forever	130
30.	On Your Marks… Get Set Go	134
31.	Opportunities Slip Away	137
32.	Paint a New Picture	140
33.	A Place for Me	144
34.	Purpose Achievement	148
35.	Reflections	150
36.	The Ripple Effect: Making an Impact	154
37.	Submissions	159
38.	Success Walks In	163
39.	Teaming up with Possibilities	165
40.	There Are No Quick Fixes	169
41.	Times Change	171
42.	Today Is the Day	174
43.	Walk Beyond	177
44.	Walk Like a Warrior	181
45.	A Living Series Talk- Contrast and Hues	185
	Acknowledgements…	*189*
	About the Author	*191*
	Glossary	*193*

Foreword

Inderjit Kaur has come through dark places that would leave the rest of us running in fear. That makes her precious outlook on life that much more remarkable. Writing from these dark experiences, she has produced a trio of soul stirring books certain to incite even the timid of spirits to be the best one can be. Her work has positively affected my life in more ways than I can count and I believe it's imperative to pass along the importance of the work I'm introducing.

Inderjit Kaur has created two other wonderful motivational books, *Living a More Meaningful Life* and *Elements of Life*. But if you only have time for one, keep *Kaleidoscope - Colours of life* close. Inside these pages she has produced a masterpiece of hope and inspiration. I have discovered the Holy Grail of a peaceful life in this third volume. Colours of life is the guidebook to the successful, happy existence I have sought for a long time now. Forever linking colours of the rainbow with spirituality, wisdom, confidence, peace optimism, compassion, and courage, Colours of life makes it possible for everyone to construct a vibrant foundation on which to build a strong, bright future.

Paul Hollis
Best-Selling Author, The Hollow Man
St. Louis, MO.

Author's Note

Kaleidoscope - Colours of Life.

Kaleidoscope - ***Colours of Life*** is a tapestry of suggestive and poignant thoughts and ideologies that serve to be your guide at any stage of your life.

Interlaced with threads of experiences of life and lessons learnt from them. Seven inspiring stories depicting the varied emotions have been woven into a magnificent array of a Rainbow. Pearled with the symmetry of success that each protagonist has achieved in this event called life.

Charting the various shades of life, the book further highlights the ups and downs of each of the characters, who are embedded here as a metaphor for a rainbow, in the patio of a plethora of circumstances. Each person has made his choice in the given situation and then lived that role with utmost sincerity, giving his life an upswing towards happiness and contentment. And that is why the rainbow serves as a metaphor for each emotion.

This book is for anyone who is ready to live their life to its true and meaningful purpose and to its greatest potential.

Thus sharing wisdom, experiences and insights, Kaleidoscope - Colours of Life intends to deliver a message that will inspire and empower the readers to sense happiness and contentment, and help them to navigate life as a true and confident individual.

One courageous step which becomes successful, encourage the next step or the journey to begin. With my book, I intend to spark a hope, and inspire all those who are entangled in the adversities and are trying hard to extricate themselves from it. There is always light in the end of the tunnel. I found mine during my trials and tribulations and I intend to help you see your silver lining in the dark cloud, with this book. Being positive and believing in oneself, inculcating a little of confidence within, keeping the faith alive as you simply flow with life, are triumphs over suffering. And that the failures, hard times, are actually assets of experience you go through, for they come to help you grow into what you deserve to be, make you brave enough to live the life that you dream.

The colours of life pages the accounts of my own experiences, stories told by other people and the thoughts that I dwelled on while travelling through the times of my hardship and adversities, which just harnessed my true potential and discover the real me.

Thus, now I wish my readers to get all the courage to manifest what you believe is right for you and all the courage to explore the real you by discovering the need for a personal change.

Inderjit Kaur

Introduction

When the idea of Kaleidoscope - Colours of Life was still developing in my mind, I rediscovered that experiencing your existence in each moment instead of reacting to it or being defensive to an action or words that may ruin your day can be far more progressive. I jotted some paragraphs while experiencing the toughest times that came to reinvent me. Being calm, even if it is an unpleasant experience, you do not allow yourself to be imprisoned in the long chain reactions of thoughts and skilfully mentor the causes that trigger stress, and harm you.

I was questioned, at times, about my writings when I was going through my roughest patch in life. So this is my answer to all those raising voices that claim women to be desolate and consider them to be weak. Thus I gained strength from the power of my pen that helped me overcome times I felt were unimaginable as well as unmanageable.

The third book in the *Living Series* is a *Kaleidoscope* to the life as the light it cast is more intense which witnesses to the most profound human experiences that I metaphor as Rainbow.

Life is full of sufferings and is never easy. No one is spared and no one can escape either. But you need to see things distinctly and this ability clears the path; making you identify all that keeps you entangled. There is no other way but we need to keep flowing like water; accept, adapt and redirect our life, thereby rediscovering it once again. Through self-awareness, we can regain lost attention and ultimately free yourself from the tangles of life. Once you unload the burden of darkness whole life starts to dwell in possibilities that brings harmony not just to your life but to everyone around you.

Kaleidoscope - Colours of Life. Part A: - Colours of Life. This segment caters to 7 assorted short yet inspiring stories that I compare to the colours of a Rainbow. These stories provide the readers with a mantra to never give up!

Part B: - Contrasts and Hues caters to 38 chapters on key words like inspiration and encouragement, motivation and positive approach, personal development, leadership, goals, lessons learned and personal experiences.

Patience helps you to endure all troubles. When you reach a stage where the only option left is to release things clinging on you and pausing your life, you feel enlightened and no longer a victim. You experience your mind is at ease even in difficult situations and this remarks you to a point of self-liberations. Simultaneously, you are blessed with more skill; mastering your potential and making yourself wiser every day culminating you to self-transformation that goes beyond transcendence.

Inderjit Kaur

13th September 2015, Mumbai

Part A
Rainbow

1
The Spiritual Violet

An old man in his 70s repaired leather bags and jackets. He had lost his wife and three-year-old son in an accident long time ago. Deeply hurt by the shocking incident, he became a rebel. But finding no solace, he surrendered to God's will and accepted that death was the greatest truth. The grief which had assumed the form of anger, took the form of a search for inner peace. He began to stay content with what he had and resigned from a big company post a tragedy in an elevator that took away his left arm from him.

Snatched off of everything that life had in store for him, he now stitched and repaired bags and other leather goods, and remained content by serving water to the birds.

He also tried to keep himself in high spirits through his selfless service to humanity. He spent his leisurely time by singing devotional hymns and songs in the temple in a bid to quench his spiritual thirst. Today, he is no longer bitter with life, has no regrets, and feels content withal he has.

He named his shop, Suraj Bag Shop, after his beloved son and welcomed his customers with water, tea and biscuits. His hospitality was relished by each visitor. In the background, one could hear Sai bhajans and Shiva Strotas that would uplift one's soul and make a visit to his shop memorable into a truly divine atmosphere. He had no complaints and no regrets now from his life. Just a smile on his face and selfless help. He spends his leisure time singing devotional hymns and songs in the temple to satiate his spiritual thirst.

This account dates back to more than twenty years ago. I was pursuing my studies back then, but these incidents have had a lasting impression on me that I wish to share this wisdom filled lessons from Jeevan kaka's life, with my readers, who I acquaint with *Violet; the spiritual colour of the rainbow.*

As usual, I was getting late for my chemistry practical and to worsen my frustration; I found that my college bag was torn. On my mother's recommendation, I entered the dark and gloomy shop, and reached the first floor, which was rather deserted.

I entered through a corridor and spotted an old man, almost a septuagenarian, cleaning, wiping and oiling his sewing machine. On seeing me, he welcomed me and offered a glass of water and brought some cookies on a plate. With spiritual songs being played in the background, the mesmerizing aroma of incense sticks encompassing the place, and sunrays percolating through the window pane like a halo, which produced a majestic set up of the tiny workshop. It was more like a place of worship rather than a workshop for repairing torn and tattered leather bags.

I just kept wondering how calmly he worked and kept things going smoothly while he looked for the matching thread and then the lining for the inner side of my completely worn out bag.

He offered me a seat and started repairing my bag while I informed him that I was in a bit of a hurry.

Suddenly, he enquired of me how my dad was and I replied that he was fine.

"Do you know him?" I asked, out of curiosity.

He replied, "Yes, indeed."

"He is a hardworking man and I know about the sufferings that he had gone through in his tenure with a company he sincerely worked for and trusted in."

I was astonished that he knew of my father's lowest point in his career. "That time spelt the downfall for my family. Don't talk about it," I muttered.

He continued, "Beta, this is life and it can't be seamless. There have to be ups and downs. I lost my wife and my son in an accident. I also lost my job. I know your dad from the time when I used to meet him in the wee hours in the Thane local long ago as we used to board the same train daily, and I can tell you that your dad is one of the kindest persons I've ever met. I lost my wife and my son in an accident. I became bitter and angry with life. Your father's company was comforting in those days. Then I lost my arm and thereafter my job, and even lost touch with him. I found his visiting card in a pocket of your bag and couldn't help asking about it.

We come across so many acquaintances, who leave a great impact on our life. We meet, both, friends and rivals on our way, but the most important thing one has to remember is to remain careful of those we trust and truly believe. They might be our friends, but the most hurtful experiences can come from the people we trust the most. When our trust is broken, we are shattered and suffer inside.

We can't avoid these vulnerabilities when times reflect the meetings of friendship into betrayal.

Be very alert and judgmental with any excessively sweet behaviour. Sometimes, it's a faked facade to cover cruel intentions, and such behaviour should be analysed by the brain and not by the heart. People, who are pure from the heart, won't bother to impress much as their qualities would itself speak for them. As their qualities cannot be concealed and would shine through.

Be wary of people, who try to please you all the time unnecessarily. People-pleasers as they called. The most important thing one has to remember is to be on guard against those whom we trust and truly believe in.

You need to at once stop yourself from receiving the pain that you are likely to experience by allowing yourself to continue to indulge in the ill intended interest. Don't make yourself vulnerable by trusting all those, who please you or come across as to you as more than pleasant.

When someone tries to provoke you to get angry or tries to push you into some situation or problem, you don't want to be in, rather losing your temper, it is best that you just walk away.

The enemy is never just the person standing in front of you with arms and ammunition; it may be the sweetest person, who carries a dagger and tries to stab you from behind.

People keep manipulating since their priorities in life are to win or get victory over every little thing. They play games with their nearest and the purest relationships like a sibling deceiving another.

So, that's the true colour. Now, people keep changing mask after mask as the need arises and never reveal their true personality. Apparently, the world is distinctive and you have to make choices to become strong or weak and not enemies or friends. They will always be there. Here, we have to play the role of a responsible person and not a victim.

If you are yourself in such a situation and you're opting to play the victim's role, then you'll never be released from the clutches of the vulnerabilities of those people wearing a mask and playing double standards.

You're always allowed to make a choice between the good and the bad: use this very carefully.

When you choose the 'victim card,' you refuse to take up personal responsibility and you are an easy prey for the rest of the world.

Whatever you choose, make it work more efficiently. It demands a great deal of courage to make a change and trust yourself. You start making strategies which define you to be a winner; you talk like a true winner. But, certainly, if you're not strong from within and try to compromise with the situations, you will reflect defeat in your eyes and can become an easy prey for the outer world once again.

It's like behaving rebellious even if your wounds are bleeding since at least, you're taking your own stand to make a choice between what's good for your life instead of being a puppet in someone's hand. Yes, you would spend some sleepless nights not being sure of how things would work or you may find it extremely difficult to figure out the things.

You will face a certain period of life to be the most dreadful when you will brood over how you'll face the world out there but if you keep on holding someone else's hand, then this pack of hyenas would even try to take control of your breath. They will make you a victim and again search for a new prey that could be moulded according to their demand and would continue to affect so many more people.

So, the people who try to please others with their unnecessary sweet behaviour or are more pleasant than required are no less than enemies who can put to test your courage. They are more than cowards; proving their weakness by trying to be superior and right all the times, but this doesn't work all the time."

The best quotes and life lessons are now embossed in my mind and soul forever. What a pleasant start to the journey of colours of life when I dipped my brush into wisdom filled words of violet colour from the rainbow.

The colour of the rainbow could not be complete without the start and without the spontaneous acts of kindness and spiritual enlightenment shown by Jeevan Kaka who transformed from being a victim to victor.

I take my repaired soul in the form of a repaired bag, cherishing the thoughtful insights forever as I walk towards my college.

Violet is a blend of energetic red and stimulating yet calm blue. Hence, it is integrated with the combined features of spirituality, imaginations, and inspirations. Violet is one of the most dynamic colours for those who seek contentment and the real meaning of life. Through this, they can expand their awareness relating to thoughts that change one's perceptions to a higher level of consciousness, contributing in growth, peace and harmony and acting as a balance between mind and emotions. Violet inspires positivity, culminating in achieving the pinnacle of spiritual enlightenment.

"You may encounter many defeats, but you must not be defeated. In fact, it may be necessary to encounter the defeats, so you can know who you are, what you can rise from, how you can still come out of it."

– Maya Angelou

American author, poet, dancer, actress and singer.

2

Wisdom Inked Indigo

When life gets tougher, we become stronger to face it. Submission to life, as it is and without any efforts, is apparently giving up. But Blossom knew that if she got stuck now she wouldn't be able to make it for the rest of her life. There are people who just let go any situation they drown their own attitudes, justifying themselves to walk in the midst of difficulties and adapt the change for a better life.

The need to change arose since the old patterns weren't working. After the train accident, Blossom was broken as Roger was bedridden, in coma and also because she was not well educated.

Roger was a clerk in the civil court. Somehow, she tried to get a job but was not successful and the hospital and medicine bills were piling up.

At this time, courage is needed to be summoned. And you have to accept the facts rather than be in denial of the changes.

Blossom started making vegetable sandwiches and supplying snacks to the court during the lunch hours.

Seeing her dedication, one of the attorneys, Ms Khan, approached her and offered her to become the nanny to her 10 and 8 year kids as she was not able to devote enough time for them because of her preoccupation at the court.

Blossom readily accepted the offer.

There are times when we forcibly resist the pressure of life. Our resistance gets tougher when we are under some deep stress or have faced any tragedy in life and a time comes when the need and the urge to change becomes so strong that it becomes a threat to survival.

Thus, using her wisdom, Blossom accepted the job as it would help her to pay the bills and change her life for the better.

Time drifted slowly and after a few years she lost her husband. The kids became her only hope in life and they too respected her more than their real mother.

Blossom never cried; she had faith in herself and she mastered the skills of hospitality, cooking and self-discipline. She knew that there would always be a blend of happy and sad days.

Life is designed in that way but we need to remain focused and should try to reinforce discipline in our daily schedule for a balanced life along with time management to get the tastiest fruit from life.

Blossom willingly admitted her life's tragedy into a life event and did not let her get stuck in time.

It becomes absolutely fascinating when you can make a commitment to yourself to make some positive changes in your life.

Once you've polished your skills and overcome the most difficult phase, you can master all the circumstances. You can practice to live more genuinely even during the hardest time of life as you have opted for dealing with everything with a positive perception.

I generally feel that self-awareness is a constant process and one should continually seek for better options with self-talks. We do follow and seek ideas, thoughts and expert opinions, but we often find it hard to reveal what we want from life.

How much are we prepared for the sacrifices and hard work towards moving to our destined path? There are close chances when you'll encounter frustrating situations in life but always remember the master key to unlock every mushrooming issues of life is Patience. The fact that life would never give you anything for free, now you allow yourself to strongly rely on your abilities. Rediscover passion if you can't discover your purpose for your life. But equivocally purposes and goals are the various life sign boards that help you keep walking down the road of life even if the situation is confused.

Blossom had succeeded in gaining respect because she did not only work to survive but also managed to distribute love, care and kindness to those kids, who were never her own. She remained calm and concentrated on her current project and she rediscovered passion as never before thus dusting off all the unsettled thoughts successfully.

Thus she did erase her past and her present, sacrificing her life for upbringing the kids of Ms Khan.

Ten years later, Salman, the elder son of Ms Khan, took Blossom along with him to the US. His sister, Saira, is happily married. Unfortunately, Ms Khan left the world in a car accident.

So, the threads that were tied as a nanny had now started taking root in a deep relationship akin to the one between a mother and a son. Salman respected Blossom more than his own mom.

We are, in fact, made to experience hardships and growths from all the uncertainties of life. After every setback, we need to stand up and rise above the rest. Hope, faith and trust all work together leading to success. Remember who you're, believing in yourself is the root.

You have got to focus on your unique ability using your own wisdom, strength, dedication and discipline. Create your own strong and self-made strategies that can help you take powerful decisions, starting from a simple word 'no' to what so ever discomforts you. Try to refocus on the scrambled path.

Develop a winning attitude in each situation; harness your potential; explore every opportunity coming your way like Blossom did. A wisdom inked reflection of indigo without which the colour of rainbow is incomplete.

The colour indigo represents deep reflection of devotion. The most positive strength of colour indigo is service to humanity integrated with sincerity and dignified with powerful perceptions, which can inhibit you to achieve higher levels of consciousness.

"Know what you want to do, hold the thought firmly, and do every day what should be done, and every sunset will see you that much nearer to your goal."

– Elbert Hubbard

American writer, publisher, artist, and philosopher.

3
Confident Blue

Sara knew her parents were the most amazing persons on the earth and was confident that life was a bed of roses for her.

Her parents loved and cared for her and she thought that she was the luckiest person in the entire world to have such loving parents. Her life was sailing smoothly on a calm sea and she had no worries about her future. She knew that her dad was always there for her like a shadow in all the difficult situations.

Sara's dad, an engineer by profession, did manage to keep life working quite in balance. He tried his utmost to spare quality time with his family and was doing amazingly well in his job too, but he managed to keep his work separate and kept his family as his most important priority. Yet, Sara did witness some disagreements between her parents, which apparently were a temporary scald that every family went through. She feared nothing; was happy and felt blessed.

But destiny unfolded the cruellest chapter before Sara one day. Sara's dreams were shattered when she heard the news that her dad had suddenly expired in the office after a heart attack. Just a day before, everything was so perfect and neatly placed but suddenly a violent storm invaded her life, making her empty and broken from inside. The death knell was hovering over her father, yet she was absolutely unaware of it. The blast had not left any stone of her life unturned.

She felt the sudden trauma and took the things deeply. Her father's death left a grave impact upon her thoughts and she kept crying for days, quoting all to herself.

'Yesterday life was so beautiful.

Everything was so perfect,

Life was so wonderful,

Dad, mom and me- everyone was happy and cheerful.

I had a dream to study: going abroad; making a good life.

I knew my dream would be fulfilled; I knew dad was always beside me to take care of it.

But, now, life has become so unpredictable. I'm so helpless.'

Change is perhaps difficult for blue. It tries to analyse it at various levels. It thinks it over and over again and slowly tries to adapt and makes it fit in its own acceptable reality and works confidently towards this change in life. Like always, I do believe that life is never easy but like water, we need to flow. So was Sara at this juncture of life; trying to flow confident.

Coping with the void from the tragic loss of her dad, Sara was completely shattered and life was becoming impossible to bear. It was becoming tough for her to overcome that blank time and space that was filled up by her father. Her behaviour, her outlook, her faith and trust towards life was changing instantly and constantly. Every moment, she kept flickering between whether to believe or not to believe in the Almighty and she was drowned by her own thought processes and kept believing in the self-made boundaries and limitations that her life and her future was in the dark.

There's a lot of sadness that engulfs you when you face a tragedy in your life. The loss of someone close and someone whom you love keeps building an immense edifice in our thoughts and our minds. It's a natural feeling of loss. As the time passes, these feelings might fade away and usually you keep a balance of emotions and somehow bounce back to normalcy. There's something more than just the feeling of loss that is shaped into a grief when you finally get to understand that somehow you need to maintain a balance in your life over the loss.

The most important thread here is an acceptance of the fact of the loss and is a necessary step in order to recover from your grief. Sara got stuck in the process, unable to figure out what she would do in life. She herself closed the doors that could percolate some fresh air of normalcy and build a wall around herself. Change was the most difficult to accept.

But, somehow, Sara tried to focus on her studies. She had always dreamed of becoming a great surgeon. Her interest in medicine and surgery tried to get rooted and took her a step closer to her awareness of being able to come out of the self-constructed gloomy and blurry life.

She wanted to concentrate on life and wanted to add colours to her dreams. And yes, life tested her once again. She came out with flying colours by getting a distinction with 99% marks but now, there was the issue of the medical college fees. Though, she knew her mom would support her in all her dreams so that they get fulfilled but she was hesitant about whether it would work.

Somehow, Maggie, Sara's mom, arranged to get some loan from the bank and Maggie decided to work in a store as a cashier. Blue is a rescuer and, sometimes, a helper like a loyal friend and it helps to build a strong relationship to keep the walk of life flowing smooth. Blue believes in giving like water that quenches the parched soul of the dry earth.

Time flowed into years and, eventually, after walking confidently on the path of thorns, Sara met her mom in tremendous happiness and she, in turn, was glad to see Maggie when she came to receive her at the airport.

Yes, the dreams had faded away and there seemed no way ahead, but Sara and Maggie didn't give up.

God's grace is always upon everyone. God is always working on us. We definitely don't want to get stuck in the devastating situations of life. But, yes, sometimes, dreams do shatter when we come face to face with life's realities. But the best strategy that works here is acceptance. The sooner we accept the truth and seek out the different possibilities to cope up, the better tomorrow is weaved. And when this happens, God is the only hope who saves us; cares for us; picks us up, rekindling our broken self and we continue to live in confidence.

God would never let us live alone. Sara wondered, at times, how God could have done this by leaving her alone when she needed her dad the most. She wasn't prepared for unseen, unpredictable and unexpected trouble awaiting her ahead in her smooth life. But Maggie soothed her troubled thoughts by making herself believe that Sara had to walk confidently and had to keep flowing like the blue waters. In the process, Sara's dreams got repaired and repainted with a hope of new life.

Blue seeks peace, blue promotes mental relaxation, and it reduces stress levels like water that calms the thirst of a tired traveller from the scorching heat. And blue does certainly delivers a sense of calmness similar to when we lie on our back and look into the bright blue skies.

Sara could ultimately walk confidently, caring for her mom.

The colour of rainbow is lifeless without the confident blue Sara.

It always seems impossible until it's done.

– Nelson Mandela,

South African Revolutionary Politician and Philanthropist.

4
The Peace Maker Green

This is a short story of innocent love. There was a blind girl who never accepted herself and hated herself just because she was blind. She did not appreciate anything in the world. She just hated everything and everybody in the entire world except her loving boyfriend. The only colour that engulfed her was black: her fiancé, her love, the flowers, her tears, her emotions, her laughter and anything she ever wished for. Yet, he was always there for her in all her mood swings and all possible travails. She believed in him more than she believed in her parents and he too cared for her a lot.

Once, she wished how amazing it would be to see the world and decided that she would marry her boyfriend only if she could see the world. God was, perhaps, in a mood to grant all her wishes and one fine day, someone donated a pair of eyes to her that made her see everything. She was so immensely happy to finally be able to see her dearest boyfriend, but when the astonishment phase was over and the boy asked her if she would marry him now that she could see the world, she was shocked and disturbed at the whole idea of it as after finding out that her boyfriend, too, was blind like her. All her intense and passionate love vanished like a spirit at this realisation and she refused to marry him.

Her boyfriend was broken hearted. He burst into tears and after some time he narrated his pathetic condition to his closest friend and requested him to write a letter to her on his behalf: *just take care of my eyes, dear.*

Thus, here the boy is the peace maker. His heart is filled in love and gratitude to the brim. He goes out of the way to bring happiness to the eyes of his beloved which is natural human instinct and tendency. This is one of the emotional colours of life- to do the best for the one we love the most.

So was the case with Peggy, who was raised by her father, Thomas Carter, as she had lost her mother as soon as she was born. Thomas was left all alone after the demise of his beloved wife and was unable to come out of the trauma caused by the sudden death of his wife. He was so shaken by the tragedy that he went back to his workplace and worked till late night in his office, trying to percolate a way out of the disaster that wretched day had caused. He was walking back home, not knowing how he was going to cope with the stress.

It was raining incessantly. The sound of the pouring rain was only broken by loud and heavy thunders on that darkest night of his life when at a distance, he suddenly noticed a dog with a defective limb crossing the road to find shelter from the heavy downpour. In spite of its three limbs, the dog managed to cross the road amidst the heavy thunder showers. He too tried to take shelter at a nearby bus stop to wait for the bus as there was not many options available at that moment since the water levels on the road were rising. This life changing epiphany showed him a breakthrough to manage the hardship of life. But there was something more that life had to teach him as he again found the dog trying to relocate from under the tree to the safe under desk of their bus stop. Now, there were two of them in the darkest thunderous night waiting for life to get a tune of peace. His heart was crying as Mary had left him alone that morning and, perhaps, this time god was also sad and hence was singing a dirge along with the rains and thunders. He wondered what would be the fate of the little child and how he was going to take care of a motherless child? That was the longest night of his life and he thought of committing suicide but the innocent face of the new born kept haunting him. He was feeling more like a disabled without Mary. But the innocence of the dog's eyes revealed an electrifying statement and he was compelled to answer for what he was running from, "I do need to face the fact and move on."

He was taken to surprise after a while when the rain subsided a little, he found the lame dog running to the other end of the road and trying to scan a dark corner under the tree where it had taken shelter for the last couple of hours. Thomas was flabbergasted to see that it had held a small kitten in his mouth as if trying to protect the new born. He looked in the corner of the other side of the road and was taken aback to see a dead cat lying in a pool of blood that might have been the result of some road accident a few hours ago when it was raining heavily. Since the cat was lying dead, he tried to call the municipality to remove the carcass of the dead cat. Meanwhile, he was curious to know what was happening at the other end near the bus stop under the shade when he spotted the dog, who had managed to carry 3 kittens safely from the rapid downpours into the safest place in the world. This just changed his perception forever and he promised to his late wife, Mary that no matter what, he would raise Peggy with all the enthusiasm and become, both, a mother and a father to her. That night changed him forever and he gave Peggy the best education possible along with the best athletic coaching available. He tried to devote all the quality time to her his pretty angel grew into a beautiful woman. He too promised to live and grow in peace. Thomas now realized that nothing in life was so bad that he had to take away his own life for it. If the worst comes, one should drop everything as it is and start all over again because god gives a second chance to everyone on this earth. A deep and overpowering depression could be lifted with just a glance at the disabled dog, who managed to save three lives in that dark rainy night.

Thomas Carter promised in front of the picture of his beloved wife, Mary Carter, that he would do all he could to make her child the happiest person in the world. He never married again for he wanted to keep his little angel away from the black fears of being with a stepmother or her stepbrothers and stepsisters. Thomas made up his mind to move to some other place. He stepped out and turned back to have a last look at his home but it felt no longer heart-breaking for him to sacrifice his beloved's memories for the sake of their love that was alive and breathing in the heart of little Peggy. He felt it was meaningless to cling on to the people he had loved once, but who were no longer there. He rested his head against the window of the cab, holding his little angel and wondering what the next day had in store for him, why this had happened to him, and was there something he could have done to save the life of Mary. All these questions haunted his mind and he felt such a tremendous pressure that he felt that his head was going to explode. Even the thought of Mary sent pangs of pain to his heart. Tears rolled out slowly from his eyes and it felt like a reverie. His heart pondered painfully of the nightmare from which he wanted to wake up and find everything just the same as before but he knew it was all in vain and that the reality was that Mary had left him forever. Uncontrollably trying to get himself together, he heard a tender and the sweetest voice knocking at his heart, "Dad, dad, I'm here." He saw Peggy on his lap, lying so calmly as if he was the only world to her and the amount of serenity and secured feeling with which she trusted him made him feel the responsibility.

He felt the responsibility. "Life is a test," his mother used to say. He was raised up with these words that kept him motivated. She always made them go to the church on Sundays. It was she who reminded him and his brothers and sisters to be grateful to god in every situation and taught them to pray before meals, which he still did. No matter what travails life presented to them both in good or bad times, they never felt alone. "We are always looked upon by god," were the words that kept on repeating as he finally entered his new home that evening. After that day, he never felt alone. He stood strong to all the turmoil while raising Peggy into a beautiful woman. Call it a golden bond or the priceless words of his mother, it always kept him going amidst all the pains. He inculcated in Peggy to become a strong believer in god and taught her not to feel that if something didn't work now, it did not mean that it would never happen. He was proud that Peggy was mature and stronger from within.

So, what now anchors the flow of life depends on all the choices we make. It becomes difficult for some people to express the warmth in their daily work places and even while in family. It's all because they are not more responsible like others. They relate themselves to more insensitive qualities of ego. Unfortunately, they drag these emotions throughout the life. They follow the traits of the unkindest life acting like a victim to the circumstances by choosing only to be pessimistic and being more defensive and would like to argue for most of the time. They tend to crave for approvals and need to be liked by all while being the most ungrateful person, constantly remaining impatient. This is never going to solve any of the burning issues in their life. Taking on the positive thinking and being optimistic works for the most peaceful growth.

Time passed and Peggy grew up. She pursued her graduation in fine arts as she practiced painting and was creative right from her childhood. Later, she was married to an air force pilot who loved her immensely. Together, they painted the world pink in love but it was Peggy's hard luck that within three months of their marriage, Peter had to leave for his duty with a very brave but heavy heart. They waved a tearful goodbye but destiny unfolded its darkest night on Peggy when she received the news of a mid-air crash and the accidental death of Peter that made her entire world and dreams shatter into more than a million pieces.

The kind of pessimistic thinking is the greatest challenge which stands as the Great Wall of China confronting personal growth. One keeps blaming the destiny or making others responsible. We just try to project ourselves to be a victim, giving up the controls of our lives but Peggy was strong in those grave times when she was raised alone by her father with positivity. The legacy of being patient and rejuvenating in peace from within was a quality that was passed on to her by her dad, Thomas, who had witnessed enormous of ups and downs in his life.

Victims love to complain and try to seek sympathy, spreading negativity and failures in the process. They try to constantly get self-approvals and self-pity. They relentlessly blame the entire world for their failures. They are simply more interested to play the victim card and accept fears as their only companions. They run away from responsibilities. Thomas took the responsibility of Peggy, stood firm which seeded confidence in Peggy too and which helped her to cope up with all the uncertain incidents throughout her life. Some people create happiness while some carry it; some just try to be safe, to be away from happiness trying to play the role of a victim throughout their life in order to get a constant attention and sympathy. Some people decide to stand in a pile of troubles without making the slightest effort to find out the best solutions, while those, who are in a bigger mess, grab a shovel and start digging new possibilities as they know moving through the issues is what that will lead to the solutions and, perhaps, to the best possible answers and self-discovery because if a problem has been created, a solution has also been made, but the only difference is that a very few realize the fact.

Somehow, Peggy's father consoled her with all his words he had but was unsuccessful as the news of Peter's death led to a tremendous trauma in Peggy which led to a miscarriage of the love knot between Peggy and Peter and simultaneously the unending traumas made Thomas gets a severe cardiac arrest.

This time, Peggy was left all alone to face the world. But she promised to herself that she would never give up.

So, standing alone on the sea shore, Peggy promised to her father, her mother, and her beloved and to the only left over sign of her love that left her before birth, that she would fight the battle and that she wouldn't give up. Excuses are never the same as reasons which are usually the outcome of out of control, while excuses are created and often controlled by us so it's better to opt for a perfect reasoning over fears and finding the best remedies to start things working no matter what or when you have reached a fag end. We must walk to reach the destination; we can never by lifted by the plane while standing on the runway; rather we have to board the flight. That was the best decision that Thomas Carter had ever taken to move ahead while he lost his wife. The same history got repeated and Peggy too decided to move on even stronger than and as smooth as peace as the confidence grows stronger every day in patience. The four corners of a stone that makes the base of every life are in being mindful, being positive, and not being afraid. The power of positive thinking is a great thing for almost every situation of life. Fear is a natural reaction that takes us to truth: the fear of how would Thomas raise little Peggy alone was a truth as he thought he would be unable after the death of his beloved but he had a chance of witnessing a dog with three legs doing its best to safely relocate the small kittens, who had lost their mother, made Thomas change his perception to become a reformed person. Life on the whole is a journey where you meet your edges over and over again. You have got to expand a little every time, increasing the resistance to cope up with the earth thus becoming stronger inwards, facing everything that is growing every time like the beautiful green foliage of every beautiful leaf we see on every stem. They edge out so gracefully, growing more beautifully to the fullest every day, reshaping the plant and gifting it an elegant look.

Perhaps, the most important gift is the choice that we make, so whether it is of wearing which colour, taking which path, walking which lane, eating what we like or make a choice from among the options we have created sometimes. So, probably, it's the choices that we make that make the entire difference. Each of our lives in all is the total accumulations of the choices we make on our way of the sombre walk of life. It's the power of choice that makes us ordinary or extraordinary. Thomas had made a positive choice when he witnessed the three legged dog rescuing the kittens on the rainy night while thoughts of self-destructions overruled Thomas that night but the life changing epiphany made Thomas to make a positive choice to withstand all the travails; to stand firm and raise his little child to the best of his ability. He had decided to shoulder the total responsibility while he had little Peggy in his lap when he chose to move to a new place and start his life again. Whether he was dealing with depressions or financial crisis, he no longer held anyone else responsible. He made himself hundred percent accountable to what so ever came on his way and obviously his circumstances started to change.

Thomas Carter and Peggy skilfully overcome every obstacle in their life, growing and making peace and this colour of rainbow nurtures life amicably.

Green is the colour of growth, the colour of balance, the colour of peace, the colour of a balanced head and heart.

It restores all the positivity back. Emotionally, green is a positive colour that loves to be an observer, a councillor encompassed with mental clarity. Green is generous with stable looks for being recognized and gives strength in persistence to stand firm in adversities. It possesses sympathetic restoration, self-reliance, stability, being down to earth, nurturing, being adaptable, nature-lover, calm and family oriented.

Green represents growth, harmony and hope. Green rejuvenates when one is physically and emotionally drained off as it is linked to the heart. Green urges too as it nurtures and helps us to see the situations from different angles and encourages materialism.

"All the adversity I've had in my life and all my troubles and obstacles have strengthened me… You may not realize it when it happens, but a kick in the teeth may be the best thing in the world for you."

– Walt Disney

American business magnate, cartoonist, filmmaker, philanthropist, and voice actor.

5

The Optimistic Yellow

"An optimist sees an opportunity in every difficult situation," is a famous quote of Winston Churchill.

Gift the fire of motivation and hope to enormous people out there.

It's almost easily understood with a very simple approach to some of the world's toughest unsolved puzzles:

What's being positive? What's being optimistic? What does optimism mean? Well, if I say, "Do you dwell in yesterday and keep stressed all the times? Then, probably you're not living."

You're stretching life, unknown to the fact that the time is slipping away from your grasp. You don't simply realize that you aren't living a life in its true sense and what is available, but are just breathing under certain terms and conditions.

Being positive is as simple as how you react to situations more specifically: reacting to the problems with confidence and self-belief. Those, who can erase all those unwanted, diminishing and dominating negative thoughts, are skilled and optimistic people.

Swarna Shakti led a very cheerful life in her early twenties when she passed her senior secondary and appeared for competitive exams. She later worked in the police force for many years. Her positive attitude was reflected in her work, home and around. She chilled out by narrating stories of her chivalry and her teams' bravery, fighting with the thieves and the criminals.

Strong inside and outside, her visions were clear; her thoughts warm and energetic and always was a cheerful person at heart, in spite of being continuously industrious. She hardly enjoyed any break in her tough job. Sometimes, she even had to miss the flavour of major festivity for the sake of her duty.

She never regretted this, neither did she complain. Often, she remained grateful to her husband and in-laws for being cooperative and understanding.

It was not that her life was an easy flow as after a cardiac arrest, her husband passed away, leaving her alone at the age of 45.

She never gave up but rather accepted the tough challenges that life had in store for her, taking care of each and every thread that was to be maintained for a balanced life between home and job. She got her daughter married, who is now well settled.

Shakti continued to remain the backbone for the family until the day she heard the most heart breaking tragedy of her son, who had become one of the victims of a train bomb blast.

Nitin, who was almost 25, was alive biologically but had drifted into a state of coma with half of his body paralysed. He was strapped all over onto a wheel chair for his physiotherapy rehabilitation after all the injuries had been healed.

Deep wounds still hurt but Shakti did her best in taking care of him like a small baby. She stood as an example to the saying that 'mothers are the best creation on the earth.'

She was doing everything for her ailing son; right from feeding to sponging, to taking him to the hospital for his physiotherapy and counselling.

Swarna Shakti, was an apt name for her since she walked the rough terrain of her life like a valiant mountaineer ascending the most rugged terrain.

This couldn't have been possible if she was a pessimist. She faced all the challenges that life presented to her by being strong and trying to accept the situations as a tough test.

Nitin could see her mother working on him right from the day the accident had occurred. Day- night- years had passed but Shakti was still walking the path of optimism with a hope that one day Nitin would stand up and lead a normal life like the others.

Her life did become difficult after the death of her husband. Oceans were stormy and, at times, there were thunderstorms, but she didn't give up. She kept walking ahead, taking responsibility in acceptance and found new possibilities and solutions to the problems.

Now, the most important thing that was changing was her process of thinking. She straightened her crooked thinking of being a victim and started flowing in the race of emotions. She asked herself if it was necessary to surrender oneself to become a slave of emotions.

"No I can't. I can't stand at the same place and get rusted."

She programmed her self-worth with the self-belief even the day her name wasn't in the promotion list. She bravely faced all the difficulties that stood as hindrance in her life being hopeful, being positive and being optimistic.

Shakti refused to give up… like the saying goes- 'when you're inside a ring, defeat is not getting knocked down but defeat is refusing to get back in the ring again.'

Shakti kept her life going by maintaining a balance between her workplace and family with her optimistic approach.

What made her see the silver lining at the end of the dark tunnel was her positive perception and an earnest urge for the life with an apt attitude.

A ray of hope kept shining amidst her thoughts and in her actions.

She had made a perfect choice between a stagnant lives and flowing life no matter how many speed breakers confronted her at times.

At times she drove slowly but didn't ever give up. Speed in life wasn't so important for her but the directions were and she opted for a purpose filled life with an optimistic approach.

A person who has a very hazy image of his or her life's purpose or rather who sees no purpose in life keeps struggling all the times and gets delved deeper and deeper into negative feelings. Those who can see the purposes or set up their goals in life make their best efforts by sacrificing their own desires and also their own life to enlighten others' and they find solace and happiness in the go. They do everything that is humanly possible only to see a smile on another face. These are very energetic, optimistic and blissful people who really shine brighter and brighter in any sphere of life and feel contented. They believe in god and know that hard times can never remain forever. They see in everything around innumerable opportunities. They know that an island can never face storms forever and beyond every cloud there lies a silver lining.

It's a natural human instinct to suspect that the other side of the bank holds all the peace and tranquillity. They're born to make a difference in the life of the people surrounding them. They become the role model and contribute every day to their life selflessly. The imperfections and hurdles in Shakti's life were embraced by her with immense courage. Shakti accepted her fate with more optimism than before.

Each and every one of us is here on this earth for a reason; to serve the purpose of the Almighty. For long, there has been a wrong belief that's been circulating in our lives: "To make a difference you need to be special and perfect." I do not agree to this statement as I feel every individual is special with his uniqueness and potential.

Unknown to the fact that something much better is in store for every difficult situation. Despite imperfections, we can still make better choices living life with a purpose. We can start a new beginning a new dream always. The only reason we do pursue our dreams at first place is that our egos want us to, they believe we can accomplish great things and desire that greatness to win. And this little victories do allow us to gain a momentum and with each little win we feel more confident in ourselves.

Swarna Shakti did understand that moving through the difficulties would lead her to the growth and lead her life with a true purpose and elevate her level of confidence. She didn't surrender to the circumstances; rather she faced every challenging situation with a smile and a strong heart and in confidence.

She shouldered the responsibility of becoming a ray of hope for Nitin, showcasing an infinite 'never give up' spirit of a mother.

The colour of rainbow is dull without the optimistic yellow Swarna Shakti.

Yellow is the lightest hue of spectrum which helps create enthusiasm for life also does helps elate self-confidence as its more related being practical and logical thinking rather than being emotional. Yellow is uplifting, offers hope and is cheerful always looking forward to life in optimism and positive thoughts.

"History has demonstrated that the most notable winners usually encountered heart-breaking obstacles before they triumphed. They won because they refused to become discouraged by their defeats."

– B.C. Forbes

Scottish financial journalist and author
who founded Forbes magazine

6

The Compassionate Orange

The most incredible thought that you have is how you can express your emotions while still in the course of life, simultaneously wearing a graceful smile. Everyone is fighting a battle of their own behind the mask that we can never understand but we can still share a word with much more compassion. How miserable is the moment when the loved one looks at you without recognizing who you are, and this loss initiates the immense grief of losing the loved ones forever. It might seem to be the most devastating situation. You may encounter the pain of dementia, i.e. how the loss of memory plays the foul evil. This pain you have to stretch lifelong with immense courage, passion, compassion and in fact the loved one who is right in front of you may be having lots of trouble in resolving his or her emotional display which may deeply break at times; where you may feel the slip of loss further away. Then, you start all over again without giving up.

The most powerful emotion you experience is when you deal with the daily chores of someone who has lost his memory. You feel your life is lost in caring for him 24 × 7 and you feel that the person you once knew is lost forever and every day you make immense efforts to make a new beginning all over again.

The other most difficult emotion is forgiveness. What causes pain in you can be restructured, making a difference in making a good choice among the adversities. I found myself getting exhausted in emotions and pains but I found the courage to make a different choice. This was the most depressing moment of my life. Wiping the tears from my eyes and acquiring a little more courage required, I made a promise to myself that I would find a better way and break the chain of violence and emotional traumas that the unspeakable acts had caused. Perhaps, I didn't know at that time how I would go about but I made up my mind, 'No more of these pains in my life' and I was about to choose a life of peace and a life of happiness.

"In the midst of winter, I found there was within me an invincible summer. And that makes me happy. For it says that no matter how hard the world pushes against me, there's something stronger –something better pushing it right back."

- Albert Camus...

How responsible are we? Being a victim of times, do we accept or deny?

Perception matters in about whatever we opt for. The choices we make are what we achieve on our way. What we treasure matters. Are we happy? Are we contented from within? We keep on finding flaws in our life and we discourage ourselves.

But there are thousands out there who sleep hungry and there are thousands out there longing to see the world.

We got to make a choice of becoming a victim or are we responsible enough? I often see people debating the topic that if someone crossing from the middle of the road has lost his mind or those students nowadays with earphones plugged in meet unwanted and untimely accidents. Now, who is a victim and who is irresponsible? What if people fall sick from the carbon emission from the mills or factories, who were healthy but now are victims? Are they responsible?

It does matter a lot. My mind is desperately seeking the right option to find out who is to be tagged responsible here? We just need to change our perspectives. Some of us are those victims who have been unnecessary dragged in. We have got to recognize how the challenges of someone's life may inspire us to look at life in a different way.

We have to be responsible for our own thoughts which are very essential for a peaceful living. Few days back, I paid a visit to my mother's house and while I was excited to see her, I was also feeling guilty as I was unable to visit her in the past for a very long time. While standing in the kitchen, helping her to make some tea, I could spot my aunt entering the drawing room and I could recollect a rough picture as I saw her after a decade and I was indeed surprised to see a woman in her late fifties very unknowingly walking behind my aunt. She arrived straight at the kitchen and awkwardly looked at me. Perhaps, she was curious and through her gestures, she queried my mom, 'Who is she?' My mom replied, "She's my daughter."

I had never seen her before so I just assumed that she may be a neighbour or a guest in the neighbourhood and did not brood much into the matter I continued making tea and pouring into the ceramic cups. But there was yet something more for me to get spellbound as I saw that as I filled one of the cups with tea, the woman lifted up the ceramic cup and her laser sharp eyes scanned the kitchen for a saucer. To help her, I gently lifted a saucer lying on the side shelf and offered it to her. Lifting her drooped eyes, she said, "I like tea, give me some more later."

I managed to say, "Okay."

She tightly held my hand and said, "Give me some more tea later, I like tea."

Shocked, I gently released my hand from her warm wrist and said, “Yes, sure.”

As I poured some more tea into her cup, she was indeed delighted and the smile that lighted her face was filled with peacefulness. What I did experience and witnessed is beyond any description. Later, I came to know that her name was Annette and she had been new in the neighbourhood with her very old, septuagenarian and almost bed-ridden mother.

She had been taken care of by St. Paul’s Shelter Homes, a mission that runs a charity to help many homeless and they also run night schools for children on the street.

Her mother was a nurse in a hospital and after retirement she had no choice, due to her growing old age and her asthmatic diseases that had made her even more vulnerable, but to be taken proper care of by Annette, who was indeed very childish though had crossed her fifties. St. Paul’s Shelter Homes was always the right place for many of the mentally and physically challenged individuals who needed a motherly shelter. They not only executed care, compassion and kindness in various forms but also assisted many with everyday living by teaching them different activities to cater to the livelihood like cooking, stitching, painting, personal hygiene, computer basics and many more relevant short term courses, so that each of them could lead a responsible life which eventually left an individual with a peaceful life that was balanced economically.

The scattering of hopefulness amidst despair was indeed a commendable work of the shelter home. They ignited a spark of hope in all the so called gloomy lives of the children, who were under privileged and left on the streets for the human scavengers.

Annette was a very healthy, balanced, normal and very much like any other happy and fun loving school girl, but the traumas induced by her father made her vulnerable and left her in this pitiful situation. Being an irresponsible and cruel father, he changed the life of Annette forever by crossing all the levels humanity.

The father's cruel nature could be traced back to the incident when his factory was shut down and he was left jobless for more than 3 years. It drew him towards the consumption of alcohol and out of the blue, he started thinking that his daughter was unlucky for him. As expected from a boozard, he just pinned her to the ground and kept abusing and assaulting her with his leather belt. He further tied her with a rope and proceeded to strangle her. Then, he forcefully threw her onto the wall that made her half dead. At a very tender age of five, she was left there in a pool of blood and unconscious when her mother rushed her to hospital only to find her condition critical where she fought with hell in the I.C.U for over 5months and came out of it as more than a challenged child. The horrific act on this little angel had changed her whole life permanently, damaging her brain for the rest of her life.

The story of Annette left me shattered and I wondered how a father could be so irresponsible, cruel, inhuman and insane.

I was feeling guilty of my opinion initially when I had looked at Annette, who was desperately longing for a cup of tea, and I was indeed ashamed of my attitude when I saw her arriving in the drawing room hours before I knew her pathetic tale.

This changed my perceptions as to how an innocent life can become a victim of unnatural inhuman acts, but still there was neither any sign of anger nor complaints regarding life in her. Perhaps, she was above those emotions.

Here was a person who had every reason filled with anger and resentment and yet I could see the intensity of life that had outraged all the gloomy shades of her childhood. She had just happily embraced life, living in to the fullest, contented with just a cup of tea.

I wished I hadn't allowed myself to be judgemental to feel the fear and uncertainty at the first place when I saw Annette with her ruffled curly hair, eyes drooping out and eyes still connecting me and asking, "Can I have some more tea?"

This encounter was a subtle reminder to me from god that some perceptions of my life still needed a refined finish.

As I did finally learn that everyone around us teaches us some little lesson. "Give me some tea," these words though were sounding very impractical as Annette tried to scream in between with her loud laughter ending with her words, "I like tea, give me some more," yes, were very uneasy to hear at that time when I did not know her as a person and thus God taught me a small lesson of acceptance of whatever we have or whatever we are gifted with. All the compassion I could see in her eyes with no complaints towards life and, thankfully, I was able to learn from this event the importance of recognition and perceptions. Annette could not enjoy all the happiness, the normalcy of life, could not even marry and lead a normal life. Here was a life that had all the right to get angry with what life had snatched away from her but she was filled with a life of patience.

Only where positive suggestions are helpful, you can range from mundane to the dramatic issues, nevertheless, sometimes, the factors depend on how much we want to accept and how much more can we do to make the change required. Positive suggestions enable you to conceive more constructive thoughts, adding more creatively to the defined layout as it outshines all the small efforts made. They can help you live more comfortably amidst all the ups and downs of life, enhancing your responsibility and to help you control better all the actions and reactions and to make the necessary changes required. Emerging to be more realistic and filled with optimism is the best way out for many uncertain aspects of life. Happiness is a state of mind where good life is cultivated more towards prosperity.

Don't be afraid to take a long leap. You can't cross a chasm in two small jumps. The most important aspects of our life are our thoughts. They are small packets of energy, active thoughts are active energy that concentrate your thoughts with a concrete purpose and make it happen by concentrating more into positive actions. This does wonders and enables your active and positive thoughts with reasoning and the purpose will get filled with positive results.

Acknowledging the travails or restraining the adaption for a change is human nature. Denial of the problems might suppress your feelings of instability for a while but deep within you, you know you're in a crisis, so the best way is to face it instead of running away from it.

Eventually, we do accept the truth and the unavoidable circumstances and try the best options available to cope with the crisis. While some day you may feel, "Yes, I can cope up," another day you are overwhelmed with the unending saga of the pains, anger and feel the loss, simultaneously you start to prepare the key inside that you need to accept the cycle of pains; endure to the last of the best option and yes you overcome the fear.

The care giver who deals with the person with dementia finds himself overfilled with the constant need of their presence and may have to devote all the time and attention. You are forced to cut back your normal life in resentment for the care giving of the loved one who is entirely dependent on you. These times are more testing and indeed tough for you to cope with your emotional self and the one who sees all this. To you, with his or her innocence filled eyes you have very less time for yourself now. This is incredibly appreciated as it's all your efforts that you are devoting to one more life selflessly. Whatever stress you encounter in the process vanishes with a simple satisfied smile of the person seeking emotional support and all your selfless love.

At times, you feel that you too are in dire need of emotional help from your friends. This may be sometimes too scary but these thoughts are the emotional waves that are trying to drift you along with making you strong enough to cope with all the traumas and stress.

The human brain is capable of handling the responsibility as much as it gets. Endless tiny decisions may creep into the brain. Sometimes, the heaviest decision may leave you completely exhausted but the immense bond and compassion may overcome all the flaws.

Taking care of someone, who is already at a loss of his memory, may slowly end up in you losing your self-esteem. This can be the most painful experience, the emotions triggered in handling them is not as simple and as easy but being a little more compassionate and a little more positive attitude may render all the potentials needed while taking care of. This can immensely help the seeker to feel contented as he or she may trust only you in the entire world and you may be the world to him or her.

Orange colour compassionates always on the go for life, warm hearted optimistic cheerful inspirations, self-encouraging and stimulating. Orange helps emotional uplifting during difficult times as the colour itself aligns as compassionate, rejuvenating us and bringing positivity in our thoughts.

As one of the most powerful gifts we do have is the ability to express our emotions, it is simple to wear a smile gracefully like Annette and show compassion to others makes the rainbow more vibrant and complete now.

However, it's not always easy, we all have our own battles to fight and we do hide ourselves behind a mask. Yet, a smile and a kind word does makes a larger difference.

"You go on. You set one foot in front of the other, and if a thin voice cries out, somewhere behind you, you pretend not to hear, and keep going."

– Geraldine Brooks, Australian-American journalist and author whose 2005 novel, March, won the Pulitzer Prize for Fiction

7

THE COURAGEOUS RED

My dad was a strong man of vision. An engineer by profession, he was an avid reader of books. It was he who planted in me with a thought whenever I was low or gloomy, especially during my graduation years, particularly in the wee hours. I still remember myself sitting under a vast mango tree or on our terrace when dad used to bring tea or coffee saying, "Indu, where there's a will there is a way." Yes, I had never ever thought too deeply about the quote, but later, I tried to delve deeply behind the words and the impact was as solid as rock. I tried my best to coach myself all the organic chemistry formulae and just kept practising a lot so that courage was a spark that ignited me and kept me going to the day.

When time and exertions of the life weathered his body, he seemed to start feeling a little low, saying that he would be living a short life and I never used to agree with him. I still remember that as a child, I used to wait for hours and hours at my door in the evening with a glass of water to be the first to hand it to my dad who had a hectic day after his whole day spent working over the fabrication copper furnace. Since his fabrication factory was far away from home, in Mulund, Mumbai and the journey in the overloaded train were the other reasons for his coming late. He used to talk about his hardships, how he had managed his studies and a part time job as a trainee engineer in Bhopal simultaneously in his initial years. He had to work night shifts to keep the family needs going and would tell me, "Indu, life is full of surprises, never opt for short cuts. Just do your best and never ever doubt the wisdom of god. He is supreme. He knows where to place us best and where we are supposed to be."

Adjust, adapt and keep moving and smile. It is the smile that I had got as a gift from my dad, who stood strong in all the adversities of his life.

Dad believed that life has broken strings that need to be repaired at the proper time. He knew a lot of the concepts that he referred to me time to time giving examples. So, though it is that every action has an equal and opposite reaction yet we can control how much we need to participate in the scene. There was no need to catch all the stones thrown at you but you must learn just to ignore certain situations and that's the best way to live life.

I still remember that he often said, "Everything will eventually wear out, only your deeds will be remembered as a part of discussion. People will even tend to forget your name in course of time but if your deeds are good, your name will be tagged around the shining deed in the process."

I had seen him counselling couples to fix their broken marriages and celebrating Holi with his friends. I witnessed him as a true spiritualist, and no matter what his routine was, he had his times fixed for every duty: early morning he performed his prayers and in the evening he walked in the garden situated at the entrance of our house with lots of variety of trees from Asoka to coconut to mango and neem that he did pampered and cared as if they were his children. I remember myself accompanying him on his evening walks and talking for hours about how my day was and what I will be pursuing further. He read late nights before he would go to sleep and I still recollect those memories when Dad, sitting on his special arm chair, would read aloud. Mostly, he would read the mythology of our Sikh gurus and he made me understand the meanings, specially reading from *Zafarnama* and *Bichitra Natak* that was included in our holy book titled *Dasm Granth* that was written in *Persian* by our *tenth guru, Gobind Singh*, that is truly inspiring and whatever I read write is only because that seed was planted in me long back by my dad towards books. There was not a single moment I had ever spotted him without a smile. Even in his last hours, at his death-bed in a hospital in Mumbai under the support of a ventilator, he had a smile on his face.

I call him, "The Iron Man with a Magnetic Smile." We all are artists in the circumference of our own life's circle. We are the engineers who fabricate the base pillars of our life. We can express on our life's canvas by choosing the colours, making a choice and sharing our experiences with one another by questioning and participating in the marathon of life.

After a car accident, he was completely bed ridden for nearly six months. It was a hard life with gruelling days and deteriorating health but yet he smiled, keeping his courage intact. Every season of life came with troubles but I never saw him in morose in tension. He kept smiling and accepted every struggle mentally, physically and financially. He just refused to give up the sign of courage.

(See the glossary last page Zafarnama, Bichitra Natak, Dasm Granth)

We grow the most during our roughest times and, indeed, we should be grateful to be going through these transitions. Just understand the relevance and the hidden message's these hardships bring as if continuously knocking the door making you aware for the action to be needed. The hard times and adversities offer an opportunity to explore the thread that's probably missing for your growth.

There's no one spared from facing the obstacles of life. We all face them in some or the other form and yes, at times, we do feel tempted to give up but that's not the solution to any issue. When you give up indirectly you refuse to learn. Yes, picking yourself after your fall and dusting off isn't as easy as it is supposed to be imagined but much more difficult to do in practical. We tend to make failure very personal though we shouldn't and we should still aim for pursuing what we believe celebrating every small win or victories as they are just tiny boost that keep us walking through out our lives comfortably, and does we should always remember that greater victories are still waiting for us as long as we stick to them until achieving and refuse to give up. This courage that gets seeded does help to overcome all the obstacles that we face in confidence.

When you are in transition from a paused state to an escalating state there will be various hurdles which will be more than enough to stop you from attempting the task but just remember one key- never give up. Just keep going. Perseverance will get you through and you would certainly be surprised to see how much you deserved to reach your destination.

Red being a positive and warm colour exudes a strong and a very powerful energy and associating will to stand courageously to survive. Red signifies a define less energizing promoting ambition and strong determination. It signifies a pioneering spirit clubbing the powerful status of all the leadership qualities Red also continues to highlight strong-willed perception and adds confidence to those who are a bit slag, timid, shy or lack in will power.

"The price of success is hard work, dedication to the job at hand, and the determination that whether we win or lose, we have applied the best of ourselves to the task at hand."

– Vince Lombardi,
American football player, coach, and executive

Part B
Contrast and Hues

8
Accentuate Your Positive Outlook

Accentuate your positive outlook. Becoming a positive thinker isn't too hard; it just requires your focus on your thoughts and active work on neglecting unnecessary feeds of assumptions and crafting your strength by focusing on your goals. Walk the road, lead the path and think like a visionary. Be a trend and an example instead of being cliché.

We need to break those habits that break us. We thus need to focus for the change that we are very much looking for. Leave your footprints to remain a pioneer. Let your struggling times be inspiring for others too.

When we talk positively, we talk by choosing words affirmatively so that the receiver can feel the positive vibes. The words should create an aura of the acceptance of responsibilities. And that's a word familiar to all of us and that is a 'Yes'… The word speaks so much. The word accentuates the strength of being positive.

The word reflects the attitudinal signature of the orator,

'Yes' is a positive word of being more expressive and simultaneously accepting the responsibility of taking the time to perform those necessary things that need to be done. Assuming that you cannot do anything about any situation or while you are facing some difficulties, it would be acting like a person who doesn't want to walk the road and is just wasting his time in complaints.

Fears of failure make you miss the opportunities that could have taught you to craft a new personality for yourself. Knowing yourself more and rediscovering your true potential is like delving deep into the ocean and bringing out the most precious pearl to gift yourself. It's like acting again more in a disciplined manner and a bit more intellectually the next time.

Whatsoever you're good in, do it more confidently and in a bolder way. Craft your strength to your best potential and enrich yourself.

Lead your path, don't walk on the old road that's already been trodden by almost every traveller rather be an explorer in life. Become a new pathfinder and be a trend setter.

One of the most important facts that need to be explored and reconsidered is the limits we put across ourselves. Just remember, these are entirely processed and designed by us exclusively for ourselves and not for others to follow. Thus, once explored, stretching beyond the edges keeps you astonished to know how much power you possessed.

I believe that somewhere deep down, dwells a real you who is constantly fighting a way through the challenges, circumstances and life's emergencies. This may get engulfed in various forms, but the day you train yourself with more refinement and with the intent of a better performance just as the best performers do, you will meet a new person inside you. Who knows to meet all the tough challenges that life had proposed? You have to summon the one who is sleeping within you.

Just try to sneak a view of the obstacles besides the limits which are framed, which are just preventing you from attaining what you are looking for or what you have been aiming to achieve.

Analyse the road blocks that could bar you from your destiny.

Troubles are always unexpected and won't leave us until we learn what we're supposed to learn.

There's no easy way to success.

Success is the outcome of years of hard work; it isn't an overnight miracle. It's a process that takes years of devotion and is also time consuming.

There's no success overnight.

And as we reach our success and survey from the top, we see new peaks that are to be explored and scaled.

That's the brilliant aspect of life- to discover a new set of possibilities whenever you endure hardships and adversities. Suffering is like a vehicle which has to be driven from inside in order to be in peace and in patience and by using all the knowledge and skills carefully to get the best possible solutions.

Generally, those who had evolved as great performers had broken through their way amidst suffering. Those who had endured pains and travelled their life facing each and every adversity and hardship, patiently understand the true meaning of transformation or the true meaning of a change. They're humbler and evolve as it's the true guide for life's philosophy.

I experienced high and ebb tides in my life. The legal cases accompanied by broken marriage and the divorce that ensued had driven me towards unending episodes of severe migraines that would not leave me until I injected painkillers.

At one time, the circumstances shattered me into millions of pieces and eventually led my spirit to get entangled in questions and I started to decay in this pool of depression. I tried to take my life. Simply without thinking for a moment, I left the house and started walking like a loner towards the direction that lead to the railway tracks. I just focussed on the dark road as far as my vision could permit and ignored everything else that accompanied the path.

Walking in unbearable pain with tears welling down along with the face getting washed in the incessant rain, I kept walking and getting drenched. It seemed to be the darkest night and I was on a never-ending road. The feeling was like walking barefooted on fire. I was wandering aimlessly around as if I had just literally lost myself and this I was absolutely unknown to me.

Thoughts stopped flowing. I went blank and was on the verge of collapsing when I found myself suddenly weightless and fell down on the ground, but I tried to get up anyhow, taking the help of a car parked nearby. I stood in pain for long span and cried loudly.

People crossing by came to a halt and curiously surrounded me, unknown to what had happened. Meanwhile, someone offered me water but I was so stressed and broken from inside that I said to myself:

'All life is meaningless.' –

Suddenly, I heard a voice, 'No dear, just calm down, have some water and then you will feel better.' Listening to the soft motherly voice, I realized that I had received bliss of blessing. And I felt a little bit enlightened.

A chill ran down my spine and I felt a grand relief from the weight of suffering as if I managed to unload or shrug off from my shoulder a huge heap of mountain of suffering and pains instantaneously. I am at a loss of words to describe the feeling but it was divine. I was convinced till the core of my heart. That evening dawned with a life changing epiphany for me.

I confess, I did cry my eyes out that night holding my younger son in my arms. He was just 7 years old. And how could I forget that I had the responsibility of my bloodline behind who found his whole world in me.

This was the transformation.

The change had kept knocking at my door but I was reluctant to respond as I was under spell of fear. But I decided not to give up.

I started to pen down my feelings. No matter how hard it was to keep myself standing in those days, I decided not to give up.

That was the darkest night of my life but I knew shimmers of the golden rays of light would fall on my life soon.

This is how 'Living a More Meaningful Life' my debut book, originated and got rooted.

During those struggling days of more than two and a half years of the legal fight (domestic violence), I engaged myself in writing during the early mornings. I drenched in music even while performing my household chores, making sure not to leave myself alone in desolation, loneliness and sufferings.

I made a play list of some melodious songs. I brought out my pen and paper and vented my deep feelings. Every morning, in a fresh mind, I tried to provide some headlines to my subjects and briefed it in notes. In this way, I kept adding and exploring my experiences into my treasured book.

This is how I kept 'Inderjit' alive.

And I no longer felt sorry for myself since then. Some kind of divine bliss had just restored and tied up all my broken strings that day. And though my life was in a mess, I just kept smiling and kept walking.

When the time flowed swiftly through the hole in the hour glass, I eventually witnessed that I had a scope that was very positive. I found a new me in the process. While repairing all my broken pieces that had got shattered, I discovered an incredible energy which was flowing profusely with an optimistic vibe towards this meaningful life.

I now say yes, there are many seasons painted colourfully in our lives. And pains are never there forever.

If I could heal the crater of my life, anyone can survive the storms of life by just accentuating one's positive outlook towards life. Life is hard but not impossible. So, *keep smiling.*

Remember going an extra mile is an attitude and you will have to walk alone in that extra mile, but each step is to be embraced and honoured while keeping an eye on the destinations.
- A living series

9

ACT WHEN YOU ARE STUCK

Clear the fog and be more optimistic

"When I look back on all these worries, I remember the story of the old man who said on his deathbed that he had a lot of trouble in his life, most of which never happened."

– Winston Churchill

It's important to recognise the changes and act accordingly before it's too late. Sometimes, you get stuck in the adversities of your life and try hard to keep going. You get closer to depression and feel like losing the interest on your life. The journey through depression and beyond requires a balance of action and acceptance and is also essential that these are provided through external stimuli. I've witnessed people surrendering to the negative phase of life and giving up even when it was necessary to give a try to overcome and to cope with depression.

Surrendering to the circumstances and getting stuck will only pile up more of exertions and you unknowingly recommend yourself to the limits that were designed by you yourself that hold you back keeping your self-esteem very low. You have to act positively and consciously to release yourself from the places and circumstances that keep holding you back. And for all this, it's very essential to live in present being in hope that still things can be worked out, it's never the end until you decide to give up.

As the demand for a change propagates more, you will witness that the complex issues that surfaced up are being cleared off one by one and we get closer to make a difference that's indispensable. Now, the change starts remarkably when you give up, the old habits of delaying the things, we thus surpass the most evident factor that keeps us getting into stagnation and that is we transit ourselves from non-performer to an active participant, irrespective of the outcomes but willing to erase the old habits of delaying the actions and all the work that was needed to be completed. This act of overtaking the old habits of delays into active participation and being positive makes an immense difference for the desired change that had faded away since long, thus clearing the fog and making the path clear for you to focus ahead in life.

The first step towards a positive attitude during this phase is to recognize the negative thought provoking demons and the demons of fears that loom far larger during depressions.

We can actually perpetuate the powers of fear by just recognising them early and fighting back as soon as they are traced.

Just as the demon of fear can go, so can the demon of hate, disturbance, and anger; the demons of uncertainties, the demon that screws you up from within and makes you lose your confidence and the list goes on.

We have to shake ourselves free from these demons that pay a visit every day, which I screen as more likely to rule and limit our lives making us immobile and keep restraining our positive outlook towards life as a whole.

The more you get engaged in the negative manifestation, the more you invite the demon of delay that keeps you fixed in the same place. The delays of keeping your project off or accumulation of thousands of pages to work on that project but not done in proper format has to be finished, or finding yourself stuck in the kitchen watching your dishes that have been piled up in the sink, or the delay in discussing the important topics with your kids, and sometimes delay in getting up early in the mornings that could have made your day the other way round and more productive.

The best strategy that one can follow is to be outrageously more energetic inhabiting little more courage and adapting to be more physically active and avoiding being a victim to endless lethargic moments which can be utilised for the transformation and progression towards a more amazing life. Just a little bit of courage can trigger the momentum that is required to keep the spirit going after a long series of hardships and struggles that you did face while fighting back the fears, you can actually witness yourself celebrating the rejuvenation thus you do meet a new of yourself more brightened side of you is explored that has now accelerated the positive outlook towards life and your perceptions are now changed that marks the remarkable difference. Using the optimism as the major tool, keep walking forward from where you got stuck. You can do it.

Depressions and negative influences can be used as an engine that can propel you to move ahead try to look out of the frame and understand the message hidden inside the hardships or the things that make you hold back and keep going ahead from where you got stuck. Getting up early then having some thirty minutes for yourself does help to provide you with quality time management habit thus you get close to fuel some more positive outlook towards life. It does break the fixed patterns, giving you the opportunity to explore more in life and getting you acquainted with a new you, who is now determined a new you and who is able to cutback complexities of depressing energies that kept a road block at your progress in life towards success and prosperity.

Though it appears a little hard and you would be struggling initially to break the old habits by adapting the new habits of active participations, this is the real challenge of life to accept the challenges that life so much demands and we just keep delaying unaware to be losing all the experiences that we may attain during the process which can fortify our lives further. A start, a beginning is needed that can change the entire scene taking you to move forward and the best is yet to come, the rewards of doing the things that we kept delaying and got stuck in time are palpable as you see the rewards immediately which adds as an energy booster helping you gain the momentum in life. You find yourself asking more from life you would require more time s you started to love your life feel free to congratulate yourself as you defeat all the inner demons with your positive conceptions and confident moves that finally made you attain all that you so much deserved. Cherish the pleasure of success and keep this moment as a package of energy that you may use whenever you feel low.

If you are tested, you are being perfected as every next level of your hardships demands a different and a stronger of you-

Keep smiling – A living series

10

Appointment with Future

We often cross the line from being disappointed to being dissatisfied with life. Usually, we do expect our dreams to come true and eventually feel dejected when things are not working according to our expectations. We often forget that this giant wheel of expectations was created and crafted by us, against the current facts and figures, unaware of what future has in its store for us.

When do we cross the line between dreams and reality? Do we really find ourselves guilty or do we blame god for things not happening according to our expectations?

Well, the reasons can be many. Sometimes, we expect a mail but feel vulnerable at not receiving it on time or we are in a hurry to get to the work and we find important things yet to be finished first. And, sometimes, when our dreams shatter or disappear, this indeed becomes too hard to comprehend and digest and we immediately seek answers and are quick enough to understand what could have been the outcomes if dreams would have been true, we get dejected when your prayers go unheard in spite of countless hours of prayers, yes, then we do get disappointed. We cross the line and start feeding negative assumptions which may never be true. We feel dejected and we start playing a blame game in the name of destiny or fate.

And we all do cross the line at least once in our life if not many a times, don't we?

Honestly confessing, I have. I've been through this phase. I've been controlling myself from screaming and leaving the faith in god. Yes, I was disappointed with the judgement of god; I had expected a lot and tried to get appointments in the future and when the appointments weren't kept then it often made me feel dejected and this forced me to deep pools of negativity and I was emotionally down. But, somehow, I decided to search for the reasons and seek the answers to my 'Why' that was successful to diminish my faith and I lost all hopes towards life. I searched the main cause to the disappointments as always it is framed don't expect so that you are not dejected but my concept was a little different without letting my expectations go low or let them get faded away but I figured out how to respond to life in a more positive way even if expectations aren't met. Yes, I completely changed my perceptions in brighter side of life for searching not the 'Why' but, 'Now what?' How to solve the troubling issues, what is done is done, now I just need to find next probabilities to match the best solutions.

Though I had issues with god for not replying to my prayers, I did learn the fact that every time I was denied, I was directed to a new set of opportunities; this redirected my path towards a purpose filled destination throughout life, which made me learn to face life the way I was supposed to face. I did experience that whatsoever life projects in form of hardships or troubles because god wants us to walk on the tougher path making us more strong that our lives demands us to be probably because god himself wants us to be stronger emotionally to get fitted in the tougher world outside.

Often, people say that all that happens has a reason behind it while my optimistic psychology forwards a different note altogether. It's like a game of pinball, where either we win according to our expectations or we don't, yet it can't stop us from playing it. It's something like a dart, which once thrown might hit or might not. As we are aware that life is not only about a win or a loss, it's a process that we need to understand. Life is a successive journey, but that doesn't mean that we get disconnected with God when things aren't working right. We have to accept some life realities we got to accept the harsh pains of defeat at times as this defeat will fortify all the potentials and the courage that was initially missing.

Life is in a new form of test always, and we do forget to thank god in this fast paced life for the blessings that are bestowed upon us every morning as we get up to embrace one more day into our life. We forget the blessings that god showers upon us even without us asking or praying. God is always with us for us. God is available and always approachable. We need to be grateful to him rather than unbalancing our faith or disbelief in god.

Don't lose your temper being angry. Getting annoyed is very easy and anger is just a step away from danger, so don't lose your temper while being disappointed or while making appointments with the future. And nobody can make you angry until you decide to use your response in anger and actively participate to the provocations or the actions from the people who are just energy drainers. Life is available now, so live it every moment. Since we think that god has let us down when our appointments with future aren't met or when we do not attain a satisfactorily result we do have that feeling. We feel god has failed us but it's not the truth god is always there leading the path in front for us to walk with ease. God has woven a dream for everyone and he takes care of all his children walking along all the difficult times, sailing us through the stormy oceans and does help us to attain what we so much deserve. You can rightfully count and build trust even more strongly and affirm yourself an appointment with future.

If god takes away something from our lives, it's only because we are redirected into something different that will add more meaning and purpose to our lives.

"I trust god and that he cares to design each and every expecting desire in his will. He knows the best way for me and I trust Him. I do believe in god's grace, his will and his wisdom. Hence, my appointment with the future is safe and serene. Now, I do walk on the path of life progressively and in positivity.

Being sincere towards your faith and being patient towards your results makes a tremendous change in our lives as I know god would arrange all the broken pieces by giving them a new form, much better than the original.

Keep smiling – A living series

11

At the Right Time

Before we experience a great success in life, it's very evident that we have to face quite a deal of failures, setbacks and disapprovals.

Feeling disappointed, we search for the logical reasons and shift our focus towards something trivial that's not required. Apparently, success is the next step forward away from failure and to be more precise when defeats overtake the drive, it's easy for many of us to become an escapist and just question the unexpected events that have occurred.

Now, we have got to remember that success is always a step beyond the failure that was eminent. Quitting is far easier but it takes a great zeal to understand the importance of the efforts that time had dedicated and the focus that had remained at the core of every goal.

People give up and surrender just one step before their cherished goals even if stocked with the best resource, the best skills, the best of knowledge and the best of expertise in various fields and focus. It's all the tricky play of the determined mind-set and will power that does the miracle. Life is imponderable and, indeed, we haven't seen it appearing in note of instructions. Life does play all its inevitable cards and no one can stop this.

It's the right time that keeps the chords playing with the melodious tunes. The force can probably enhance your performance like an elite is thus not ruled out by any chance.

Yes, but I do again add a suggestive thought here that along with the performance, it's a blend of desire, will power, focus, persistence, vision and strong self-belief. Now, once the desired concepts are generalised, it's essential to work out the best way by presenting a layout format that could be conceived finally into action. Persuasions to the right directions and moving forward in confidence, it's a time now to crystallize the proposed changes and expect the desired results.

The moment you conceive the thought that you no longer wish to stay in the place where the growth of your successful life is just stunted and decaying, it becomes the turning point of your life.

Perhaps, there are various reasons when one chooses to steer into a new direction.

It may be your work, your family, your relationship, your job or your career- anything.

The point of reference here is once you trace out that something isn't working and you're stressed about it, the need arises to opt out the greatest change.

At the right time, opportunities do knock at your door and constantly keep giving you a wakeup call. When you're in the transition from a paused state towards an escalating state, there are various hurdles fusing in the obstructions which are more than enough to discourage you from attempting the task, but are constantly fuelling your desires to convert the challenge and change the things that need to be polished and craft your strength.

When you're determined that you're willing to take all the efforts precisely, it's this thought that signifies your desires turning into reality. Now, the concepts are not mere thoughts, rather you're willing to put all your efforts by sacrificing the favourite leisurely world and investing your valuable time to grab the opportunity in order to fulfil your dream. It's the right time now and you're doing your best by identifying the opportunities that knock on your doors. Now, you find yourself working positively and converting your desires with defined purposes and at this right time, something important happens that's created by you for you that can mark the change or, more categorically, marks the U- turn of your life. Persistence and determination are fused now to bend that is opposing to make an inappropriate and untimely appearance from different directions. These are the distracting cards that are being played by life and you have to handle these situations very delicately so that your determination and focus are not shattered or missed from the destinations that you are aiming for. As opportunities have sly habits of slipping away sometimes, you have no option other than to remain vigilant at this time.

People give away just a step before the flag point. This is the right time when your patience is tested as sometimes success does wrap itself into delays, discouraging you so much that you give up just before noticing the silver lining.

Quitting is the major cause of many discoveries, which are yet to be explored, as defeats overpower the mind-set that was once determined has now become lethargic. Everyone commits this silly mistake but we can play safe, can't we?

If we are aware of this card which life plays and do not give up, we are sure embracing the greatest success which would be a true success that would be unshakeable during any storms of life. Being committed and being determined, you're more eligible to mark the greatest calibration of success by finding the opportunities at the right time. Remember, if you're stuck between opportunities and vulnerabilities don't feel sad as these are all testing times tempting you to quit and surrender.

Don't forget that these testing times have to be faced. Accept explicitly that you've to complete what you had started facing all that bars your path of success bravely and undaunted. Keep putting one courageous step forward to another as these times are surely coaxing you to gather valuable experiences and is presenting you with a wonderful asset called PATIENCE.

Keep walking and keep the trust, no matter how hard life is right at the present. You have to pass through this dark tunnel until you see a tiny little sparkling ray of hope. Don't quit before the last step. Your destination might be just a step ahead but the biggest mistake we often commit is quit at the last moment. Don't do that and repent the entire life.

The rougher the path the smoother is the cream of the destinations. So, go through all the experiences and valuable lessons that life teaches you to become more skilled and a tougher warrior, who is ready to face all the uncertainties of tomorrow. And work hard but make it look easy as it's said that a bird must first learn to walk before it takes its flight towards the vast expanse of the horizon making sky as its limit. Remember, one successful courageous step encourages another for the journey to begin thus leaving your footprints on the path in your awesome voyage of this life.

So keep your eyes open and work out the best for the right time is now. The right time is not when you quit after climbing the mountain and one mammoth rock blocks your way and you just succumb to the terror of a fall. The right time is to walk beyond crossing and solving by figuring out how, when, where to resolve and attain the zenith of glory.

So, what are you waiting for? Act now! This is the right time.

With time, the things which were once impossible start to breakdown; changing and marking our path easy to walk on.

Keep smiling – A living series

12

Be a Stand Out-Craft your skills

The concept of being positive and looking forward to life through a positive lens is prospering explicitly. Everyone possesses the ability to achieve his or her goals if the desire to do so is outrageously intensified.

Everyone can reconstruct a better purpose and seek a reason to live their own lives. It's just a continuous and persistent effort and performance that's needed to be guided in attaining the purpose filled goals and to do so we need to just take a decision with a little courage and venture out from our most comfortable cocoons to tour out looking life through the lenses of self-analysis and self-confidence.

Now, the concept that's been evangelizing for so long needs to be eloquently explored.

What is self-confidence?

How do we define self-confidence and relate it parallel to self-esteem?

Why is it essential to possess self-confidence? These have morphed to become the most subjective and engaging self-help topics. And I'm determined to enhance the best way to ensure that I'm able to put some justification here.

Self-confidence is rooted when we redirect our perception from negative to positive outlook towards life.

I've been adaptive to this life changer episode very recently since I was wandering around in an aimless life just like a vagabond.

Life's experiences have uncovered onto me lots of uncovered lessons which have earlier been ignored by me.

And I did learn that when we are fortified with optimism, we are more accredited to self-confidence which germinates into a healthy plant by penetrating its roots deeper.

We are able to stand tall against all the odds. Likewise, when we say hear or read the word self-confidence, we know that we are hearing or reading about a typical self-belief where a realistic perception and practical approach is planted for getting results

Personally, I believe that self-confidence won't be alive with the absence of self-belief.

Adding a metaphor here let me quote: -

"*Self-confidence is a little child of self-belief where one is ready to take risk to achieve and that one, who strongly believes in self, will strongly believe in self-esteem and would definitely pursue or risk something that's desired to suit best of his or her abilities.*"

The golden rule that's universally morphed is that self-confidence is extremely important for almost each and every aspect of life.

Apparently, it has been observed that if you're self-confident you lose all battles of life no matter how meagre it is. Yes, believe me- almost every battle.

Self-confidence is a superb quality that's admired by everyone since it can help you to win even a lost battle. But the one who doesn't possess it might lose a winning battle.

Yet, it has been observed that many people struggle to keep the pace and lack this quality, making the circle vicious when this results in being insecure and unsuccessful in every aspect of life.

It's a great accomplishment when you are able to inspire others around you with the stories that depict your success after all those adversities that you had survived and overcome only by mere self-confidence. It's like an extended circle in which your confidence is in a different aura that literally acts as a silver lining in somebody's darkest night. Isn't it amazingly commendable?

Self-confidence is the finest of skills that you can possess. This is explicitly stated with all the success stories.

All the successful stories explicitly state that the finest skill that a player should possess is called self confidence that makes his success unique, hence making him an exemplary.

Self-confidence can be a continuous learning process whether you're polishing your own self confidence or whether you're encouraging someone else's; it's worth all the effort. As I stated earlier, confidence gains momentum and you reach where you want to reach. Confident people inspire others so whether he is a boss; client; doctor; patient; teacher or student, no matter how meagre his designation is, he would leave his footprint for others to follow. Thus, this also redirects the successful personality indirectly to a confident individual.

Well, overconfidence does take a different tangent though.

So, how confident do you see yourself? Perhaps, the confidence can be one calibre among the many different ways to add a feather to your hat. Your attitude and your behaviour does paint the picture required for you to shine in life. Well, it has been learned and experienced by me at various phases throughout my life that confident people are always ready for taking any initiative and risk. They won't hesitate to accept their mistakes as well, even if being criticised, they do graciously accept their accountability and responsibilities keeping way for analysis, and always readily accept their flaws and exhibit their willingness gracefully for rectification.

Whereas a person, who possesses low self-confidence, would always hesitate to take the initiative and would never take any risks as he is just engulfed by fears and negative impacts. They prefer to choose their comfort zones and try best to remain unnoticed after attempting a few mistakes and eventually giving up by refusing to take responsibility. Thus, this results in self-destruction as everything is conceived and manifested in negatives. They lack self-belief; they aren't sure of anything, while a confident individual always takes a step ahead towards success by believing in oneself.

So, after dispensing distinguishing accounts of self-confidence and self-esteem, let us now understand that what is demanded by our life. We need to polish our skills at every level and craft our unique self so that we can be referred as an example to be looked upon. Be a stand out and craft your unique skills, adding the best quality of life called confidence as confidence is the key and determination is the ruler.

Life is a successful journey starting with self-belief.

Keep Smiling – A living series

13
Being Committed

'If opportunity doesn't knock, then build a door.'

– Milton Berle

Every single day I keep learning and feel better as I acquire more and more knowledge. You start learning in the cradle and finish at the grave only if you wish to learn. I firmly believe that we can do anything and there's no word called 'impossible.' Yes, the difference in attitude that I brought to my approach apparently is very simple as I applied optimism in my outlook and since then it never let me down. I do believe in positive statements and I find out the positive vibe in the negative statements too.

Every day, I compete with myself, expanding at the edges and working a bit harder the next day.

Yes, I do adapt this principle even during my morning walks.

Every day, I increase my walking time by just 10 minutes and also adapt the same process with my speed the next day.

Thus, everyday I've to beat myself. I compete with myself so that I can polish my skills strengthen my performance and all this just needs a disciplinary approach and determination. Instead of life, I'm more interested in the importance of life. The key is recognizing the opportunities life has in store by taking a less travelled road in spite of hardships. In fact,

I believe in creating my own path rather than following the regular one so that it becomes an example.

Most people draft their goals but add the spice of delay and make it lose its brightness and then it opens up the gateway to failure that clouds the progress. Just remember that hard work and sacrifices would pay you in the long run. All you have to do is push a bit more and don't give up easily; keep trying; remain committed to your goal and focus on the proposed thoughts.

Focus on your resources, focus on all the positive qualities that cross your way and focus on your skills. You just need to find a better purpose and cause to fulfil your passion in life. Take a moment to examine the clutter that's the sole reason for your unhappiness and your unsuccessful life.

Everyone needs something that keeps them interested in life that provides them with a purpose and automatically leads to personal growth.

When you are stuck between the emotional traumas, there's a feeling of unhappiness and stagnation revealing a lack of purpose reflecting your low esteem which had developed during the time of difficulties. Be proactive and remain committed to your cause if you think you can. Try to figure out issues before hand if you are aware that certain things could've been differently approached and there is a chance of things getting messed up.

Thus, you're saving your precious time in the process if you are able to foresee. Keep yourself motivated via news articles or blogs which inspires and motivates and depicts positive approach. Learn from your mistakes and be committed towards your goals.

Vision has something related directly to your dreams. All the greatest achievements were once a dream; once a vision;

once a desire that were later designed and the dreamers with their strong dedication crafted their skills and determination and after pursuing their dream or vision ultimately made a success by implementing them into reality.

Poets, writers, sculptors, painters, sages, composers or musicians whosoever had a vision had got it reflected in their works. They designed the architecture of the beautiful world with their vision and had turned their reverie into reality. Remember Columbus, who had a vision to explore new lands and new places and a new world, set out on a voyage.

Visions are the seedlings of reality that are conceived by the dreamers.

You need to cherish your vision and ideas just like you cherish your favourite music that drapes the purest form of feeling; that regenerates all delightful perceptions. This perception converges to such a point that transforms your thoughts to quench your desire more about what you're looking for.

You can acquire what you desire but you should dare to dream.

The greatest accomplishment was when a tiny little thought was born in your mind just like an oak sleep inside the acorn dreaming to grow huge someday and just as a caterpillar waits with patience in its cocoon or a nestling waits inside the shell of the egg.

Yes, circumstances may bring unfavourable conditions but they shall not remain the same for ever you see. Everything changes. Every little thing needs a change just as life is a constant change.

But you have to be committed to your goals, your dreams and your accomplished thoughts to get the desired effect. The ultimate key line that we should inculcate is that we must cherish ourselves and be happy with our self-worth instead of leading a life as similar to a weather vane which selects a mode of movement only when the wind blows. The driving force is being positive and being a positive doesn't mean that you have to be stubborn and unwilling to face life realities. All I want to emphasize is just cut back complexities from life, choose simple ways and the ability to acceptance to even all the negative phases and turning them to your best capabilities with your solid determination and perceptions because it's human tendency to keep delaying instead of solving issue that can be used to constructive bridge to walk upon. Remember that all the positivity and the positive thoughts that you breed and live in would certainly enable you to perform the best even in the worst situations. Being you, and being committed, you can build up a strong wall of self-realisation and with self-competence every day you can overcome all the barriers as quick fixes does not give long term solutions. Yes, but the truth holds true that being positive works in progress helps you to be responsible further helping you to set meaningful life goals.

Craft your strength and redefine your unique self.

Keep Smiling – A living series

14

Being Responsible

Hard times draw us through difficult phases which redecorate our lives with incredible gift of lessons. Nature is an amazing teacher. Life is run by 'Nature's Rules.' You must have observed the collection of cacti in the desert that bloom magnificent array of flowers. Life is like those cacti that have to live under the harshest conditions but the moment the conditions of life becomes congenial; it blooms flowers through miniscule happiness.

Pearls are derived from the great depths of the sea where lies tonnes of fatal dangers similarly good times in life are like those uncertainties that the rough conditions can bring to the shore like precious gifts.

Life can be hard. We all have to go through our good seasons as well as difficult ones. But hard times bring many blessings as well as are equally important to strengthen us from within by fortifying the perspectives in the form of self-awareness and turning us to be courageous on the go. Just be determined and let the burning passion of achieving your goals glow like the fire of the Sun.

Some of the qualities of the very best leaders that have walked before us are to be screened every time you're in difficulties as they would supply strength.

No one was a born as a leader. Nor was one born an artist or a writer. They created their path and changed destiny simply by practising a little more of their passion, devoting the best of their potentials every day, stretching a bit more routinely at the edges and working hard beyond capacities sometimes.

We grow the most human during our roughest times. So, why do we judge these difficulties in our life as disasters when actually these times introduce us to ourselves? We get to understand our strength and weaknesses only during these difficult times and for me, the difficult phase of my life was my greatest teacher that made me acquainted to me, whom I hardly knew otherwise.

Hard times bring in transformations by challenging pieces of our lives and help to remove the difficult phases after which we can feel that we are truly alive. These are the times that always bring tiny miracles but you can feel only if you are receptive to those senses. Your decisions, your likes, your dislikes, and your circumstances all get reflected in your personality.

You will be able to control your surroundings, so choose them wisely.

Rechannelling things you are associated with and the choices you have been profoundly segmenting for a period of time can eventually shape your thinking and actions. These would finally shape you overall depending upon the choices you make.

Sometimes, it's hard to embrace and digest when our dreams shatter and the immediate question that triggers the brain and makes you restless is 'Why?'…

It is then that we start to analyze all the good and bad outcomes that are unavailable by then and that are by the time overshadowed by vacuums of all the self believe that we had once clubbed in the process.

We often intercept with… 'Why did god postpone my happiness??' This question is inevitable. Truth remains that god is still working on us to place us on a better path. We need to closely connect with him and believe in his wisdom. Sure, we might have missed the opportunities provided at a point of time but don't leave an inch while complaining what we have been deprived of. But at the end of the day, we need to be RESPONSIBLE. We are work in progress. We are given another great day in life for fulfilling all that we want to. Just be grateful, accept to be responsible, work a little harder, look forward towards your goals with an all determined mind set. Problems can be the cutting edge that actually distinguish between success and failures, rise above stretching the edges, practising more a little inn determination and devoting more to your work no matter what it is just make sure you give your 100 percent performance by sacrificing a little more to be applauded and be distinctive in the crowd of the competitive world.

Avoid complex daunting issues with simplicity, by being patient.

Keep Smiling – A living series

15

Blissful State-Mind, Body & Soul

Take a little voyage into your soul to ensure that you're living life to your fullest potential. When your mind, body and soul are synchronised, then you're entitled to the key benefits of peace, happiness and tranquillity and would reach ecstasy.

Incredibly stressful life and modern gazetteers have made the lifestyle unbalanced, creating a total havoc. People lack relaxation and due to tightly schedule daily chores and fixed routines, they are on the verge of bursting out and desperate in need of breaks. Which means that the balance of life is missing that indirectly triggers many unresolved and unpredictable issues leading to an unbalanced society and family. It's time to take a pleasant initiative by making a difference in your life by opting for some disciplinary action. Harnessing a healthy lifestyle; eating healthy food; practising yoga like deep meditation and breathing techniques can all together bridge the gap. Defeat the hectic scheduled life with a step up to walk towards positive living that would be accompanied by eating healthy followed by yoga. It's not that hard as assumed, it's rather just a matter of a little determination besides a disciplined mind-set, and you're surely going to reap a brighter harvest of a healthy and peaceful life.

Aware- Awake- Arise- Adapt- Acquire-Accept.

The daily encounters with our stressed life and modern lifestyles do need a balance of positively enriched thoughts accompanied by sound health. We need to distinctively explore the areas that are relevant to be worked upon, right from the work place to home to personal relationships as well as family. After detecting the imbalances, we need to start the journey by taking one step ahead right in front by adapting some of the best choices and making it a habit of trying to attain an elevated state of mind in order to attain ecstasy. Let me assure you that it's possible. There's no need to spend lavishly on expensive spas, gyms or recreation centres but just scan around yourself relying upon your eyes, only then would your environment supply you with all that you were looking for. It's very important to relate and response to the stresses that triggered through the things we have been neglecting since long. A very little effort summed up with a little bit of desire and a little bit of discipline and you can do it too.

Relaxation, breathing, light exercises, walking, music, reading good books, consuming healthy food, drinking enough of water, gardening, swimming but keeping away from energy drainers and negative people and things by switching off the gazettes that connect us to the social network during weekends and donating quality time around family friends and your kids would definitely bring you a healthy lifestyle. Re-decorate your workplace or living room with flowers, incense sticks, candles, bright coloured curtains etc., to summon the positive energies. The same technology which gave you the gazettes to run instead of walk does also provide the pause and reverse button, so use those simultaneously. There are on and off keys on each and every gazette. It's not at all necessary to be their slave. Simply put off your laptops, cell phones and the 'idiot box' i.e. the TV for some time. Make the best use of this time to rejuvenate yourself naturally. Shortly you'll observe that you are feeling elevated by attaining a state of bliss and happiness. Practising yoga is not just a workout; its internal cleansing and attaining the state of bliss; it's like adapting a healthy lifestyle and nowadays, it's become a style statement that the healthy and wealthy follow. Yoga is not just about working out; it's about a healthy lifestyle. To initially instigate your nerves, start with deep breathing and focus only on your breathing part. Inhaling a good amount of fresh air is like fuelling oxygen to each of the million cells in our body that energises to activate and maintain a balance of the body-brain by removing toxins as waste. It's like you clear all the emotional clutter that all the uninvited thoughts that were troubling you, keeping your mind occupied are now relaxed. Yoga helps you to be more focused, more in peace and you feel energetic throughout the day.

It's a little difficult to adapt the habit of shouldering some added responsibility but it will be easy once started. It's just a matter of determination and discipline. It's like when we see a huge mountain and are tempted to climb but we are unsure whether we would be able to reach the top. Same way, once a thought of adapting some personal goals is seeded; keep working on it if you want to get the desired results.

As we put our feet on the base of a mountain, we locate few short scrambled paths that aren't clear but vague, still we try to step forward and to our surprise, we immediately get a place to put the other foot, and so the journey to clinch the uneven way starts. As it's said that every mountain has a path though could not be seen from the valley.

View your life through soft lenses like you admire the beauty of the Rose.

Keep smiling – A living series

16

Coalesced with Potentials Yet Flooded with Fears

How strange it is that we follow the prescription given by the confident doctor blindly. Again, without restraints, we believe every word of the speeches of some orator whose charismatic personality appeals us to invest our time without a second thought. We rely on books, we hear great leaders.

Yes, we are compounding the great quality that everyone admires and calls-

'Self Confidence.'

Remember, we are all a blend of capabilities and limitations that is restricted to our capacities. Most of us have got all that is required for a complete and contented life, it won't be wrong to phrase that, we are coalesced with potentials but yet flooded with fears.

Being positive and being confident are some of the brimming self-help topics evangelizing for quite a long time, which are eloquently penetrating their roots deeper into our society. Yes, it's now that we must urgently identify the loopholes that are restraining us from proceeding towards the state of bliss that we so much deserve. The fear of uncertainty and the fear of unknown results in the fear of some of the unresolved questions like: What will happen tomorrow?

Let me put it simply... if you're able to identify the crisis and resolve the burning issues without letting negative thoughts overpower and engulf you, this directly reciprocates that you're a positive person and that you're doing perfectly well, doing excellently with self-confidence.

You just need to harness your potential and be on the right path in the right direction.

Conversely, if you're finding it difficult to break the vulnerability of crisis or difficulties and you're not sure about yourself, here you're certainly under the shade of negative influences and though coalesced with the finest potential yet flooded with fears.

It is essential that this concentrated shade of negative aspect be diluted first and needs immediate attention and has to be crystallised into positivity. And when the process starts, we can immediately see it sublimate, vaporizing the fears. And you're accredited to your best shining and sparkling form to perform like elite. Well, the only things we need to check now are the speed breakers here.

We all are brought to the brim to touch the finest mark of great inborn qualities, but, sometimes, there are several speed breakers on our way and we need to stop by or at least have to slow down a bit for the journey to be hazard free and smooth ahead.

Communications, self-awareness and knowledge are the stepping stones to success. Sieving through the process, we can polish all the above mentioned skills for a better performance and brush up into better perspectives.

Look at the stumbling rocks as challenges that are deliberately designed into your life to strengthen you. These can actually do the astounding job similar and as good as a work out that keeps on toning your muscles of efficiency and self-esteem.

Always remember the simplicity in these golden key lines: -

1. 'We are capable of acquiring what we desire by setting some personal goals.'
2. 'We are capable of resolving all our problems by conquering our difficult circumstances.'

Remember, we will never experience real happiness unless we face and overcome real obstacles while we are pursuing our goals since we are all capable and engineered in that way.

People, who constantly keep fretting over the past and brooding over their failures just remarkably summarise their negative influences and draw a drooping curve of their life. More evidently, when they say, "life isn't fair and not worth living." This simply means that they have no personal goals, they lack the reasoning skills to dwell in possibilities and they have no purposes in their life. They fear in taking up personal risks and responsibilities. They're just flooded with fear, which is similar to somebody who is trying to get himself acquainted with learning to ride a bicycle and tries with all his might to balance himself on the bicycle, but due to the fear of falling down keeps standing still to balance himself and is left unnoticed to life's sealed envelopes that are filled with numerous possibilities of lessons and experiences but finally he quits without even trying even once.

The real challenge is to shed the shackles of fears and unseal the envelopes of life and move forward by paddling the cycle, maintaining the equilibrium. But yet, sometimes, engrossed in the panic of failures people tend to stand still even if they get a chance to sit on a bicycle and ride it. Hence, obviously, the ride is shaky.

When we're not sure about ourselves and surrounded by negative aspects, we are scared to go beyond any line. We stand still at one place and find difficulties to search for a new set of place to venture a new set of possibilities that is left unexplored. We are not interested in directing ourselves towards some objectives, we rather take a back seat on a ride which goes on and on aimlessly thus incorporating the route of only circles that doesn't have any end point and at the end we reach nowhere but at the same point from where it all started, hence we are back to square one.

We feel dejected, lost and realize that we were so vulnerable that we kept trotting aimlessly and became a victim of the circumstances. And then we label our life as 'Meaningless.'

Remember the short fairy tale of the shoemaker and the elves?

It was precisely the decision of the shoemaker to accomplish his goals while he manages to cut out the leather beforehand, keeping the designs ready for the elves, which appeared after midnight and actually stitched together the shoes, while the shoemaker was sleeping. Now, for a while let's imagine what if the shoemaker had not set his goals, he would have never accomplished the target of making the desired number of shoes before the scheduled date? Similarly, we need to conceive some rough drafts for our goals and pen them down with confidence to accomplish it.

We are designed to overcome every obstacle; it's we who need to just courageously rise above our horror, straighten our crooked and pessimistic thoughts which are influenced in negativity and which lack self-confidence.

Regain your self-confidence, and set some personal goals to be on the track. Accept yourself as and how you were at the beginning without underestimating your potentials. You cannot attempt to ruin yourself and stop yourself from participating because of those trivial mistakes or flaws or terrors.

A typewriter's performance with speed and accuracy can be a motivational metaphor, but do we throw it anyway for its typing errors at times due to its technical slag. We rectify and complete our drafts, don't we? Just imagine, how many saucepans must have caught fire; how many hotdogs would've been overheated and burnt, all those overcooked cakes that none dared to taste or ovens that got burnt beyond repair while the best chefs in the top class multi cuisine or five star hotels were in their culinary schools, attempting and failing but still repeatedly polishing their skills until they achieved the desired results.

I'm sure those stumbling rocks must have added an extra feather to their hats and loaded them with an asset of experience.

They gathered experiences whether positive or negative and kept walking and looking forward since every experience counts. Unfortunately, we won't realise now, but years later, we would really appreciate the lessons we had learnt from our failures. We would appreciate all our downfalls; we would appreciate all our setbacks as they were there just to polish our skills more amicably. It's just that, we need to believe in the process that is helping us to gather experience of a lifetime in which failures and successes appear in an endless sequence.

We are coalesced with the potential of adapting the best, performing the best and leaving behind the footmarks, which can be an inspiring gateway for millions of people right out there who are struggling day in and out to come out of the darkest tunnels. Let your story inspire so many and let everyone live the life that they so much deserve to be in.

"*Passing down the road,*

I did witnessed sessions of seasons

Breaking through, but whatever time was,

I walked to withstand all

As I didn't allow me to break through the times, just had a hope

That all will be fine."

Keep smiling – A living series

17

Craft Your Strength-Be You

Anything you want to achieve you can. If you desire and follow with an iron-willed determination, you will find the best possible way to reach it.

Every one of us possess the unique qualities that can be fortified by crafting our skills and with expansion of our performance when we devote ourselves and make our potentials worth and venturing more and more to make a new start today itself. Only weak and pessimistic people would fail to climb up the ladder of success.

Deep within everyone, there dwell those powers of distinctive qualities that would take us to the zenith surprising us and these forces would bring about a new renaissance.

Now, focus on your current issues and obstacles that are holding you from moving further. To make the journey hassle free you need introspection and work out all the flaws.

Interpret these road blocks as experiences that discipline and willpower would deliver till you reach the summit. Initially, these thoughts are too hard, too scrambled and we find that the change is so messy that we would drive close enough but perhaps would give up. Hold on right now and relax. No going back and just focus ahead.

We are designed to perform excellently and we are fully equipped with all the potentials required. It's just a desire and determination that plays all the cards for the wheel of fortune to change. Study says that most of the brains just remain unexplored and the point is that on an average a human projects more than eighty thousand thoughts in 24 hrs. It's amazing and simultaneously such a waste that more than 80% of these are thoughts of the past are which serve no purpose and are hence meaningless. Our brain needs a daily exercise, so that we can make the best use of the unexplored mind and must work hard extensively to expand our thought processes on more positive perspectives which add to sculpt and strengthen our life.

Focus on those issues that those accumulating terrors have clouded and occupied your brain's spaces. Fill them to the brim with pure knowledge and positive aspects. You're not here to fritter over the past failures and issues that cause pain, when you have the ability to accomplish everything that's conceived by your inner self.

We should recognize our goals and accept our flaws and work to rectify what's needed. The first step towards progress is to know the things which are yet to be learnt and to remove the areas of ignorance that are withholding you from your progress. You're not going to be strong unless you know where you're weak, so keep exploring and crafting your strengths and win over your weaknesses. It doesn't matter how many times we fail but how many times we attempt and accept the challenges are that matters.

Every time, we would learn something new that will be added as an asset to our life's experiences. Even if you accomplish a miniature goal, do celebrate and cherish this act as a small packet of energy boosters, which can strengthen your self-confidence and embed a new skill into your personality.

Self-acceptance and working towards what you possess best on whatsoever you're good in would re-invent a new personality in you. Renovate your skills by learning from all your flaws and adding your positive qualities and strengths which can be fortified, build up a strong and new person within you.

You will discover a new person residing deep inside you and would be surprised to know that this you dwelled among the horrors unnecessarily, whereas you were capable of doing everything.

Craft your strength and polish your skills. Be yourself… And just be unique- that's important. Why? It's because that will make you the only person, who can render the world with your unique skills.

So, there's no point in fearing or feeling low if you don't fit in at times. Be strong and face what's to be faced. Make yourself feel as important as everyone. Be proud of yourself since you have the ability to be a stand out. Be yourself.

The road diverged
Uncertain and vague
Eyes see blur and
Search for fate…
any way chooses
Destination unknown…
Deep is the faith, to walk straight…

Keep Smiling – A living series

18

Darkness Will Fade Away

It's absolutely solitude around me and I am all set to write about little things that matters the most.

Though it's raining and darkness is wide spread as far as I can see through the window to my left which enables me to view outside.

Rains with a full range of showers making atmosphere cool and winds at intervals significantly marking the onset of monsoons, hence making the atmosphere cool.

Dark is the night and the only sound that I can hear is waters splashing and drops clattering with drumbeat sounds on the window roof. I see thunders, lightning in between some time.

I can feel the sumptuous of the rains that delivers its fullest form marking its presence on the parched soul of earth.

Something that relates here is that no matter how hard the path is, no matter how dry was the summer's heat there's always a knock of cooling rain on the heart of earth that quenched the thirst making it prosper redeeming the faith once again in peace.

Life does make the routes unpredictable sometimes and we give up waiting as we start losing our patience and it's obvious that when you venture out on a tough path of your life. Of course, sometimes, the things become hazy and unclear and tempt you to give up.

More precisely, this hold true if you're in pursuit of your dreams with full determination and dedication.

But let me make a subtle reminder here that these negative thoughts and setbacks are just like a thought that's born out of fear and have a temporary appearance.

So, if you're a student, a writer, a musician, a chef and whether your best dish, or your manuscript, or your resume gets acclaimed or rejected or you're recognized in your field or face rejections always the cards that are playing in your mind is the inevitable storms your thoughts that can make or break you.

There will be thoughts that make you feel low, thoughts that regenerate negativity and tempt you to quit the show but somehow, you need to move ahead; you need to keep moving.

You need perseverance to get thru these hardships and the critical times that are monumental barriers between you and your goals and dreams.

Apparently, we all face these hard times and times of uncertainty. Nobody remains special to be in safe exemptions. It's very true and the fact that each one of us face obstacles and at certain time we get tired and try to give up. We quit.

Let me advise you never to quit. If you do so, indirectly you deny learning; you deny exploring your own hidden potential.

You indirectly lose the opportunity to lead a path that could have been a turning point of your destiny, leading up to success and victory. Hence, just be prepared to anything as more succinctly said that it's never late and it's not worth if you haven't been through a rough path making enough of sacrifices.

We all of possess a remarkable quality of adapting according to our best ability. We are designed to adapt the best possible availabilities; no one would prefer being unhappy unless he or she is going through some tragic incidents in life.

Adding a metaphor, comparing a human mind to a garden, which can be cared and cultivated intelligently or can be just left unattended, adhering the possibilities of remaining barren with unwanted weeds with no beauty of peace and would continue this way ageless. Finally, one day, the whole garden ends up being like a wild dry barren piece of land.

But just imagine if it was cared for properly by the gardener time to time; watering and plucking the unwanted weeds and allowing only beautiful flowering plants to grow, it would have been an amazing sight.

So, likewise, we humans should adapt this amazing quality of keeping our minds free from the weeds of negative assumptions and allowing only flowers of prosperity and positivity, thus cultivating the perfection that's needed for a balanced and peaceful life.

A human mind is capable of adapting the best quality of weeding out the unwanted negative and impure thoughts. Eventually, we witness that we are able to get the best of our lives that we so much deserve. We are the gardeners of our souls and we can guard our lives best way; we just need to redirect our life into more beautiful possibilities.

In the process of pursuing the best adaptability, we understand that we can walk through the dark tunnels and always dwell in possibilities with purposes and goals getting the desired and effective veiling into reality.

After all, darkness fades away.

We are the master weaver of the tapestry that is appearing in the forms of success and failures. We can always make best choices for the challenges that pan up and that demand a change. Darkness will always fade away.

Every today is always concluded with a hope that tomorrow would be better and that things will be fine, which can bring out the best of you; making you outrageously more confident, and the next best thing you can do is to take controls of your decisions and your priorities that get transformed into your actions and overall reflecting your personality. So, whether it is someone overtaking on the highway or someone unnecessarily provoking you at your workplace, you have to choose the best way out instead of reacting at the very first instance. In fact, you can be taking all the situations in two ways… for instance- if someone overtakes you on the road, be grateful that you were spared out or you could have met an accident or you could scream out yell out of your way but that would definitely harm you in your health disturbing you in every sense. Thus, the bottom line is that every action when reacted can have completely different outcomes.

I pray that my readers get the strength to discover more of self and are blessed with courage to set up the change that's immediately required in their lives, which could mark the presence of its existence and help them live to the fullest potential that they do deserve so very much.

Life moves in the directions of your focus, once we give importance to good things in life we get success in articulating some baseline for living.

Keep Smiling – A living series

19

Dream for Excellence

Life is a great book, that teaches all aspects from the tiny little mistakes to the most important things in our lives and sometimes, can lie to us and none of us can ever trace this tiny mischievous play of our life and it's something that, no one will ever stop it. It can play all sorts of games with us, without us even knowing, because, we can't find suitable formulas or procedures controlling it.

Indeed, life doesn't come with a handbook of instructions; it's we who have to experience it while still believing in the process called life. But whatever happens in life happens for some real reason and, perhaps, for something good. Whatever decisions life takes for us are already planned by it long before we understand. We must learn to accept it, rather than behaving as a reluctant recipient. We must come to terms with the fact that no matter how hard we try to fit in this imperfect world and no matter how hard it is to keep the pace flowing, still we have to keep moving. World will never acknowledge us for who we are as there will be some sort of opposition in every corner and at every turn, but still, we need to dream for excellence and believe in self.

But everyone wants to be happy at the end of the day. We strive hard to make our life peaceful and tranquil and continuously make effort to ensure that everything goes well. And we start making best of our inputs throughout the stormy nights, throughout the lonely days, throughout all the cold memories seeking calmness, peace, and perfection.

At the end of the day, we embrace life as it comes and it gifts us succinctly, making us stronger to live another day in stronger affirmations. Being positive makes all the things working in smooth flow. Take some time for yourself in isolation from the busy scheduled life.

Ask yourself: - "What's going on in your life, what you're looking for and how much effort you are putting in to pursue the immense purpose of life to flow continuously without giving up."

Start making priorities and dream for excellence, don't settle less than this.

Say 'No' to all the distraction, temptations and intended interferences that build up a block in your growth to prosperity. Well, until you've decided to give in your best, including hard work and sacrifices, results will be vague.

Hard work does make a profound difference and, remember, there's a very thin line between making things happen and letting things happen.

Just keep working on every little thing that helps you to accomplish your success, right from even smallest achievement, like making a difference by getting up early morning. Make life's simplest pleasure as excellent accomplishment.

Remember that the identities, ranks, titles, designations, accolades are not achievements, so don't mistake it as success. The impact and your presence that you make in someone's life and your surroundings count and do matter a lot and this is the true medal for you as a successful lifetime achievement.

Each and every little thing has a unique ability to create the difference that can make things easier and better. You've got to nurture your courage more and craft your skills and just dream for excellence, working harder, and being dedicated in whatsoever you're pursuing.

Start your journey of being in excellence; walk an extra mile; spend your positive energies setting your path; revive your resources for a better tomorrow.

It's wonderful that you're committed to making some changes and working towards something better for your life and for this you need to drive ahead with a fuel of positivity and courage.

Be honest and believe in yourself and understand that you're looking not only for a change, but you're trying to explore the hidden potentials within you. So, work towards it and strengthen your discipline. It will take some time but nothing is impossible.

Just keep flowing easily and touring the great map of life with a dream of excellence in every little thing.

It is important to conquer your doubts and fears thus empowering the success over failures.

Keep Smiling – A living series

20
Expand Your Vision

I believe that somewhere deep down dwells a real you, who is constantly fighting a way thru the challenges and the circumstances and the emergencies of life. This may be enveloped in various forms and factors though. But the day you train yourself better in the terms of performance as the peak performer do, you will meet a new person inside you.

"Nothing can be done without hope and confidence."

– Helen Keller

Look around you; there are stories before you of those who have mastered their own path walking through adversities. Seek your own path, take the responsibility of your future now and enable the expansion of your vision.

You have to willingly accept the challenges and should have courage to walk through your fears to reach your goals that are important for you. At times, life may agitate you; circumstances may influence you and give no results, no matter how much you try hard to keep things going.

You may find things pestering you and you start losing your self-esteem and self-confidence.

"One important key to success is self-confidence. An important key to self-confidence is preparation." -Arthur Ashe.

Just remember that life is a series of events and choices and everyone will have to endure the harshness of life. As we grow most from all our greatest hard times and sufferings.

Most of us are simply wading through life with an average journey whereas life can be lived to the fullest with couple of disciplines and mentoring of self-assured mind set which can provide, immense of capability to perform your everyday errands with more vitality and great results.

You can expand your vision and spark some light to the grime of the gloomy future.

Identify the troublesome issues or something that's not working. Get insights and analysis of all the conditions or situations that deflate your positive attitude or are declining your self-esteem.

Low self-esteem can relatively affect your life in every possible way, right from your home to your relationship and even including your job and health issues. But by expanded influences of positive approach and harnessing the power of your own thoughts and confidence, you can boost yourself with loads of great self-esteem. Challenge all the negative thoughts or try testing accuracy of your thoughts. Trace the plausible explanation for the situations and check out all the facts and logics. It may be hard to recognize the root cause initially but once identified, things can be figured out quite effectively.

You got to work persistently to overcome weaknesses and take a small little bold step towards your goals and you will witness things that seemed hard to pursue once slowly getting better and giving you the desired outcomes. Keep going; keep working hard; keep getting better than yesterday.

Self-confidence and self-belief can shape you miraculously, strengthening you from within and further results in growth of your enthusiasm and in expanding your vision for tomorrow. No matter how you feel today about yourself, right now, still you can opt for a brilliant you. Remember, acknowledging your current situation and circumstances is an act of strength and does reflect your responsibility that you fuel and courage you to make possible changes, accepting challenges. Make a list of the troublesome issues that are annoying you as this will outlet you to access and evaluate how you could deal and work it out. Yes, sometimes, we are encircled in some vicious circles of negative thoughts and people but the only remedy to this is ignoring them. And this is only the truth that we should ultimately adhere to, making a self-reminder every time we get stuck that we have only one life. Honouring this very basic element, we can look further in our everyday activity with a light shining that is to be followed in every circumstance. Dream of excellence and not of dying like an average person.

"All our dreams can come true if we have the courage to pursue them." -Walt Disney.

So, if you really want to experience and explore a life time of success, you just need to improve your skills, improve your performance, including strategies of self-analysis, introspection and all your thoughtful considerations.

Think about why and how your self confidence and self-esteem are important in your life. How can you improve by adopting better strategies?

Take a moment to reflect be honest to yourself. Your answers will conclude and define the directions of your life. The aspirations and your goals should be stretched further beyond your thinking.

So, expand your vision now.

When we fortify ourselves with optimism and positive thoughts, we are more accredited with self confidence that spreads its roots deeper making us stand tall against every raging storm of life.

21

Gratitude is a Celebration of Happiness

Everyone is seeking peace and tranquillity from life. No one likes to get indulged in unnecessary tensions and stressful life.

We strive hard throughout our lives day in and day out trying to be industrious; accumulating name, fame, accolades, positions - all sorts of materialistic forms of happiness but the true happiness lies deeply delved inside ourselves. When we are contented with what we have and we are able to bring a smile on the face of the person in front of us by making him see the glittering sunshine even if he is struggling hard to surf up from the darkness of his life.

Happiness often stays along forever only if we allow it to be there with us when we include it in our lives just by being more grateful and uncluttered to the world of negatives and grudges.

By being grateful, we acknowledge the presence of everyone as equally important and we contribute more towards life being less narcissistic and in this way we agree to most of what life has in store for us.

Apparently, being grateful to every person, who actually contributes and serves some kind of reasons for you or is there for you always, is appreciated.

If only you could percolate some time from your busy schedule for demonstrating your gratefulness towards your parents for they cared for you every minute in the walk of life i.e. towards the journey from your childhood to youth.

Being able to illustrate some gratitude towards your friends by showing up and remaining beside them when they needed you the most brings out the real you.

Thanking your teacher for being supportive at times and at various occasions can be just a great act of showing your gratitude.

It's remarkably well appreciated when one manages to take out some time from their busy schedule and just feels the bliss of thanksgiving. Apparently, when you notice your elders showering tons and tons of blessings upon you always even when not asked for or they constantly pray to let their children be happy and in peace and praying for them, then you must reciprocate the same through your respect. Being grateful is a sign of a pure and noble heart, and in being grateful you spread happiness like a splendid celebration.

Just be outrageously more energetic, more positive, and more enthusiastic and nothing can stop you.

Keep smiling – A living series

22
Great Influences

Negative thoughts do impact our life. They do something little more that does make an impact to our brain and body as well as to our beautiful life.

Just be there with me for some moments, so that we can cater the cards of negative impacts on our life.

Suppose, let's just imagine, that you're walking alone in an almost completely deserted road as you're unable to start your car and there's no one around. Apparently, the first thing that settles in is fear which can run as fast as you could have ever imagined with all types of doubtful events which may never happen. Further another instance, if you're stuck in dark forest and you clinch into the fears of unknown voices approaching towards you.

Immediately, your brain pans an emotion of fear which impacts to first keep yourself safe and not be worried about the world out there,

ignoring all the facts that you can perhaps opt to run or to climb a tree or immediately call your dear ones by making a call, but this life rescuing thoughts remain irrelevant in the presence of fear that has now eventually multiplied in hundreds of negative thoughts, deeply in your brain.

Now, you just focus on the unknown fear and the voice you're hearing in deep forest.

You do not want to explore the best way out of the dark forest as you're stuck in negative assumptions. You stop being practical and just get drifted in dark fears. This is how negatives influence us, almost paralysing us to move a step further.

Similarly, experiencing the toughest sessions with stressful events in life, you drift suddenly and now you want to just ask yourself how long I'm supposed to suffer you've already given up as you feel paralysed.

Well, the negative content of thoughts has already piled up forcing you to give up. The events that are becoming extremely difficult tempt you to give up.

In both the cases, your brain just closes the better options that could have been an easy way out. Both times, we see that the doors were closed due to negatively influenced thoughts that did certainly impact your brain by a simple fear of the unknown and uncertainties.

Unfortunately, in both the instances, the negative thinking blocks the expansion of ideas that could have been explored to get suitable solutions. Negative thoughts just stopped you to get the most appropriate way out. That's the way the negatives get hold of you, thus unbalancing your walk. Also, it greatly influences our brains and life. Thus, these impacts our life full of fears, uncertainties and opens the doors of unknown reasons that stop you to walk in confidence with courage.

When we don't make enough of efforts to make necessary changes, we tend to give up and allow self-made limits to our growths.

Just a simple example here would be the best way to make you understand. We all know that eating junk food won't help as we know it's unhealthy. We know that not exercising and not caring of ourselves would definitely impact life with medical issues and lethargy.

Here the role of will power is getting diminished as you're not motivated and you're not feeling good.

Thus, brain makes a recession towards negative trip and closes the outside world and you venture out in a depression. Emotional fears, anxiety, anger stress all work together, making you feel vulnerable.

Now, here's the importance of this debating issue: Does being positive help? I would state -yes, indeed.

Positive is filled with possibilities.

Let's figure out what positive emotions do in helping you to find better possibilities.

Let me put into simpler form.

Being positive redirects our minds to look for more options.

Being positive helps broadening our sense of adaptive behaviour and fuels a positive vibe that opens one's mind resulting in contentment, joy and happiness

Your experiences would improve and this would make direct impact on your skills and performance. You now believe in yourself first.

You look forward to life and your beliefs get strengthened into looking for the best choices available.

Benefits of being positive don't just end here, they further expand and double your will power and enhance your skills, leveraging resources, shaping and eventually crafting a new person out of you.

Your communication skills get enhanced; you're now able to put your thoughts across in confidence that helps you to attain the deserved results.

You tend to get support and success in life.

The exploration of better choices and better changes promote a new creative brain that gets accepted.

As stated earlier, negatives do just the opposite.

And so, it's important to understand how being positive work, does it help?

Of course the answer is:

Yes, being positive works, it explores a finest new individual in you and there's a retrieval of joy and happiness in life.

"The best fighter is never angry."

- Lao Tzu

Keep smiling – A living series

23
Keep Walking

As we see the lavish green nature coalesced with beauty, it reminds us of the fact that it could not have been possible without the determination of the seed that was buried in soil away from light but the seed knew it had to lose itself in search of light hence the seed opts to rise above and keeps adapting the weather's change standing tall refocused and determined, and eventually ready to stand marking its presence as an achievement and inspiring the world with one thought and I quote "The seed of every act springs with the hidden seed of your thought to overcome all the challenging situation with positive determination."

Keep walking, being assertive and being positive, choosing to be more joyful and happy in every situations of life.

I do certainly believe that happy people shine brighter as they dwell in possibilities they live in today; that's the only truth available now. Being happy and being positive is the only way to make a difference and keep walking.

Positive thoughts help to shape you and the world around you in success. Apparently, success means different to different people. Some are happy to gain a ranking, some may be happy to acquire more wealth, some are happy with their health.

The list may be unending but yes, if you're not positive you may create a hollow dark gap of uncertainties in the form of a vacuum that will leave you unbalanced and unexplored to your potentials. You would definitely resist taking a risk and fail to accomplish the desired goals of your life.

Let me simplify a little bit more about being positive as that's the essential and important element that keeps us walking.

Be sure that you learn from everything you come across.

Be sure that you can make an assertive decision in your everyday chart, no matter how big or small the task remains. Make sure that there's a purpose for your life that you can look forward as a ray of hope that you can clinch up to, while drowned in deep despair or hard times. Do perceive a clear vision of your thoughts that you're seeking in life. That's like setting up a goal brick by brick like the making of a wall.

Don't just set goals; set some probabilities of all the pros and cons that you would adhere or something like a backup more precisely a standby strategy if in case everything fails?

Don't hurry completing easy things; try the harder ones a try, and experience everything by taking a risk and expand your edges by performing a little extra every day and keep honing your abilities to keep walking in persistence.

Be a person you want to be, and be your own boss and your own director, expecting greater things from yourself. Yes, you're affiliated to rebuild and reform everything that is needed to make a difference. Act bold and thus rebuild your confidence and boost your enthusiasm, facing all your fears actively and positively, and in determination to defeat the negative surfing issues permanently. The more you intend to walk with courage, the more you'll feel positive about yourself.

Yes, the path will be crossed by your critics at times and you may get provoked by their remarks but remember if you receive a remark, take it positively as constructive criticism. Just do not react when you react to your critics; give them full marks for their assessments. Things will be not smooth, every path will be unclear and vague enough for you to give up and this may tempt you to hold back, but you must keep walking even if you fail; don't worry- failures are important as well. If you have not failed, that simply means you're not trying hard or not participating enough to push. Just think what you could have done in absence of your fears by adding a little pinch of confidence in yourself. Take baby steps every time you face fear or failures but just make sure you don't stand at one place and get stagnant. Keep the hopes sparking inside always no matter what and just keep going forward on and on and on.

On this Road… Keep walking.

I knew that I was in desperate need to walk out and completely break from my current path that I was walking aimlessly. I did not intend to just make a simple change to the way that I was walking but to profoundly change the way I lived and just needed an inspiring thought in form of life changing epiphany that could twist the world around me. Once I realized what the real and, more importantly, what mattered to me the most, the flame was lit and the inspiration canvassed as action. The most important and the easiest way to navigate your life is self-help.

We have to weave the wrap and wefts interlacing the threads of happiness and sorrows. It's just as simple that if you intend to make a drastic change just stop living in past and you need to prepare yourself to start new things discontinuing the former that were stunting your inner growth and entangling you into darkest tunnel and stopping you to live your real life. The peril of the thoughts that are accepted widely about life pertaining that everything happens by chance or more likely that time has not come for so and so makes me a little considerate. Yes, seeing people waiting for stars to get aligned in the skies often leads only one thought in my mind that people dwell in least purpose, I mean that they lack purposes and goals in the life.

We need to first self-help ourselves. And that is something no one else can do for you.

Just be prepared to understand that not all decisions would lead to the desired outcomes but be also prepared to all the inevitable circumstances building some sort of flexibility that simply means adjusting and refocusing your outlook into more possible probabilities and that you can now adjust to. Feasibility is established. But once you adapt or opt to quit, it becomes a habit of lifetime.

Every next level of hardship demands a stronger and different you; be prepared to face the challenges.

Keep smiling – A living series

24

Life – A Beautiful Collage

Life - A beautiful collage of challenges, adversities, happiness, courage, determination, achievements, success, struggles, hardships, process, and delays. We attempt to face what has to be faced as the rough terrain that has been laid for us to walk constantly makes us who we are supposed to be. The path embarked with lessons making us shine, polishing our skills, and making us a better performer.

You can live in the past or long for a bright future, but if you don't change for the better you may be at the edge of extinction. And apparently, what can be more challenging than to challenge yourself to improve. Perhaps, at times, things will be upside down and you may feel stuck as there will be unending issues, traumas, and difficulties.

You may be convinced that life is a disaster and not playing fair towards you. Pains and wounds would remain unhealed. Unsolved issues would seem as if you would never be able to get solutions that you're seeking and days would never seem to have an end but just go on and on and on…

Many of us would definitely just give up, but those who won't will be the winners, who will emerge as crafted, skilled practitioners and masters of their own destinations. But leverage your resources as there is growth even in failures. Thus, conclusively, I crafted some reminders out from my transitions of hardships which I wrote as self-reminders as to myself,

Confidence: It re-conditions all the unbalanced barriers, elevating your purpose of living more significantly.

Will power: Abundance of willpower and discipline can contribute fascinating performance.

Challenges: The tougher the challenges, the better lessons inculcated.

Change: Changes are for better, for growth and when you accept a change in positivity it starts a new beginning.

Peace: Peace of mind is when we are able to live in the present moment more focused, more in enthusiasm.

Choices: Ultimately, the destiny unfolds according to what we choose in our lives.

Experience: Life is: The collage of vibrant lessons, enveloped as experiences.

Lessons: Lessons are to be mastered as self-learning teaching aids.

Courage: Courage gives us self-control to perform constantly.

Determination: The dynamics of your determination makes the purpose of life more meaningful and possible. You are entitled to achieve your goals if you are positively determined to do so.

Perfection: We feel happy when all is perfect, but tiny little change creates a complexity in our thoughts at once.

Grief: We are dissatisfied often if pleasure doesn't last or if pain doesn't vanish.

Affirmations: At the end of the day, we embrace life as it comes making us stronger to live another day in stronger affirmations.

Positive: Being positive makes all the things working in smooth flow.

Interference: We will remain unhappy if we deliberately interfere in the natural flow of life experiences.

Needs: Needs versus wants can be focused and limited.

Achievement: We trade our lives collecting achievements, not aware that these are external rewards for investment of our precious life.

Patience: Patience helps you to endure all the troubles and issues thus helping you to navigate your life as a true and confident individual.

Growth: Struggling in negatives, we are actually webbing our inner selves, restraining growth of life and happiness.

Decisions: Whatever decisions life takes for us is already planned by it and we must learn to accept it. We need to constantly configure the circumstances thinking carefully to what our decisions would play in drawing the consequences. Think ethically while decision making as it should not cause any unfair suffering. When we are dealing with difficult decision making we must make sure about the negative consequences and review the benefits too.

Responsibility: Many of us don't take enough responsibility for the magnificent event called life. We make it toxic with self-created anxiety and worries. And always remember the responsibility to make a change lies in you. When adversity strikes look inside yourself for all the answers that you are seeking. Yes, indeed we can look upon to improvise all the situations if we owe the responsibility to ourselves leading the way honestly and thus we excel the life at every stage as a positive thinker.

Simplicity: Complexity can be cut back. We can make choices for a simpler life. Needs versus wants can be focused and can be limited. We must come in terms with the fact that no matter how hard we try to fit in this imperfect world, it will never acknowledge us for who we are. We always feel like becoming everything else around us. But what we do not realize is that everyone wants to be happy at the end of the day.

Teacher: Life is a great book that teaches all aspects of the most important things in our lives and sometimes can lie to us and no one can even notice or something that no one will ever stop it. It can play all sorts of games with us without us even knowing because there is no one controlling it. But whatever happens in life happens for some real reason and perhaps good. Whatever decisions life takes for us is already planned by it long before we do understand and we must learn to accept it rather than behaving as a refrained recipient. We must come in terms with the fact that no matter how hard we try to fit in this imperfect world, no matter how hard it is to keep the pace flowing still, we have got to keep moving as it will never acknowledge us for who we are.

But everyone wants to be happy at the end of the day.

Efforts: We strive hard to make our life in peace and tranquillity and continuously make effort to ensure that everything goes well and we start making best of our inputs throughout the stormy nights, throughout the lonely days, and throughout all the cold memories, seeking calmness peace perfection.

Response: Remember all the turmoil and assumptions of being defeated in your attempts while facing the adversities in life is only in our minds. Our lives are affected mostly by the prevailing thoughts and worries which would never ever happen and when things do happen they turn out to be far less daunting than expected. Since our ability is limited to control the circumstances and the external world we can still make a control on our thoughts and minds by controlling our participation in responding those events by mustering positive attitude. It's always hardship and struggles that brings out best qualities of you.

Hope: Being proactive to face every obstacles is a wise way as this dynamic attitude would open the doors of invisible to visible casting a light of hope. The night is darkest before dawn but how can we forget the rainbow after the rain!

Understanding: We understand to love, to give, to endure, to find pleasure, to please but what we do not understand is ourselves during all of this is that all the pleasure and happiness is temporary and that we are given to be happy or in sorrows as a parts of our subscriptions of our life that we deserve.

Acknowledgement: Life can lie to us and no one will stop it, it can play all sorts of games with us without us even knowing because there is no one controlling it. But whatever happens in life happens for good. Good of all in it.

Keep smiling – A living series

25

Life a Beautiful Challenge

When the day breaks with serene beauty and pleasant sounding chirping birds, golden cool sunlight scatters to each and every corner of this beautiful earth and coolness of calm breezes hellos on your cheeks as if greeting a very blessed day to you.

Do you find yourself filled in positive energy or you find yourself struggling to start your day? Though, you know the intentions are good, but still you find yourself off track and as the day progress you feel vulnerable facing challenging issues and struggles, resulting in derailing you from the main track.

How often do you face this?

Do you agree that this difficult phase will be a period of transit where you get opportunity to learn and grow, certifying you with best experiences of life?

How hard did you try to put best efforts to ensure you're not pushed back in distress? Your answers to this entire question would reveal whether you need to master the craft of self-discipline and get committed to the cause.

Life is a beautiful challenge just like a big jigsaw puzzle which isn't easy though. The pieces that are colourfully placed are structured ahead, every time we step further, as tiny or monumental problems, issues, hardships and struggles.

But you know that the beauty is to face the challenges, find solutions to the issues and problems with courage, applying it as smoothly as we apply a balm that kills the pain, which helps us to bear what's supposed to be faced and on this road, we have to search hope on the sides as it will act as a fuel making us move towards the belief that a beautiful tomorrow waits for us.

Perhaps, happiness, sorrows, victories, defeats are just like season or more defined as day and night with a continued process of change.

No faded thoughts cover the line, that indeed life is beautiful and every moment is a celebration to be in this life.

Difficulties and struggling times are there just to evaluate our patience and courage, thus crafting our true character as human being, who is ready to face what's to be faced on the way in enthusiasm.

We know that yes, trials and tribulations do make us strong and prepare us to face the challenges of life with equanimity.

The farmer can sow the seed and plough the field and has to wait patiently for the fruits, but he can't force sunlight to shine brighter or can't turn the direction of winds and rains. Perhaps, in life, there's no gain unless you bear all the pains and wait in patience.

If someone assumes that good times will be forever gets easily succumbed into pressures of challenging hard times and is forced to be pushed back into depressing state.

Believe in yourself, it's all that is needed. Have faith in yourself and just conceive a thought of self-belief in little of courage.

A thought of change must to be seeded by you, for you, within you and know that if you master the elegant craft of self-discipline now, it can make you gain positive outlook towards life and you can face everything and accomplish all that you want. Good and bad days will be there always no doubt about that but you need to be focused more and committed.

You feel now that it's absolutely amazing once you start working on yourself with a little of self-awareness. You're committed to make a positive change into your perceptions, so don't keep it under wrap.

Let everyone know you're trying to rise above the storm with self-discipline and this commitment would help you gain strength in self-belief acting as tiny packets of energy boosters.

Be committed, be honest to yourself, and craft a beautiful person of yourself. Now, just a little effort is needed and you're done. Even the strongest kings faced adversities and challenges and life was never easy for anyone. But one who knows how to weave the threads of happiness and sorrows explicitly and surge the crown of victories on their heads shine in history forever.

The ultimate challenge is achieving the mastery of self-discipline, as we all have the potential to live up a perfectly happy life.

Master the beautiful challenges of life with self-discipline and commitment; the more you practice, more it would be easy.

Like a sunset which looks more vibrant if it's covered by infinite irregular shaped clouds, enhancing the radiance of lights. So is life and without difficulties and challenges, its beauty remains unnoticed.

Because, I do believe…

'Life: A beautiful challenge` we have to keep walking the path of life somehow, facing all that's on the way as we have to go back home one day ….

Explore the hidden potentials in yourself through unseen opportunities. There is never a failure. We either learn or we are successful to overcome the difficulties.

Keep smiling – A living series

26

Life–A Series of Choices

I'm learning to trust life once more. I'm trying hard to understand, but at no point I'm letting the disappointment and uncertainties grip my confidence and the immense faith I've rebuild to trust the journey of life. I've learned that disappointments are only the outcome of too many expectations. Great things happen once we opt for positive outlook towards life.

As it's well said, there's no giant step, it's always about lots of little step that work together in one direction for the expected results.

But our life's are always imparting us harder tests, forcing us to the walk and endure sufferings which speaks to our souls and I'm hopeful it's going to rediscover our better life.

And life surely supports us always in some form of some beautiful lessons that we learn from our mistakes.

As a general idea that I do believe more succinctly is that our mistakes teach us and they impose and impact us with lessons we need to know.

And I frame life mistakes as my teacher which has the ability to induce knowledge which is available in the forum of experiences.

Thus, this teacher of my life remains explicitly original and most noble, but also as the most powerful paradigm into my account of life.

We often fear for the unknown tomorrow but if we understand and keep learning from our mistakes, there's a fair chance to inculcate a deep courage and confidence required to face the insecurities and discomforts of tomorrow. It's obvious pattern of the life that once we are habituated in a circumference of comfort and known, and fears surface up on the arrival of unexpected troubles.

It all started with my toughest time. I despaired day and night to overcome the life's uncertainties. Losing all hope in myself, I was convinced, I'm just a failure. I started to slip deeper and deeper downward spiralling in unhappiness and found very hard, every day to face the life.

I found myself losing the pace in life as everything had gone wrong.

I certainly wanted to come out of this state but wasn't sure of myself as I was gripped in my fears that surfaced on the arrival of demands from the life for a change.

I had not many options left, I had to make a choice either to be there forever and continue living with the suffering and pains or opting to stand and to raise my voice against domestic violence against me and my kids.

At times, option for ending my life seemed a very simple way out; still I'm here writing. As yes, I did go through a hell of a life. I was broken into pieces and mentally quite disturbed. Emotions were drifting in all the highs and lows. At times, I was drained out and was continuing to feel lost. Depression gripping at its best. How long could I carry on? I asked myself one day, "What I'm doing here?"

All these thoughts gearing up to make me feel stuck in the most devastating situations of life. Thus, when life demanded a change, I was unsure about myself. As all the strength and positive outlook was already faded on the way while facing the abuses and tortures in various forms. Yes, I was shattered from within. Knew nothing about how I would be going with rest of my life.

I was convinced that any attempt that I did make for a change would eventually end up into again a failure.

But one fine day when all the limits of humanity were trespassed, I received a kind of divine blessing that encouraged and filled me with all the strength needed to raise a voice against inhuman tortures.

That day, the change was sculpted and a ray of hope sparked in the darkness.

As I do believe strongly 'A boat that never ventures beyond its moorings into oceans and face storms will never get damaged but boats are not made for safe harbours; they are made for a sail in the sea. To face the rough waters, to engage itself hard, sailing against the tides and winds in a voyage to reach its destinations and at times sailing against sea winds but keeping the sail on.

So is life. We need to keep going.

The fear that was developed and that rooted deep down since ages needs to be scrapped from the very scratch, from the very base, and from where it got originated.

Remember your childhood lessons of falling down number of times in learning how to ride a bicycle.

We fall number of times while mastering the art of walking while we are toddlers, but do we stop or do we let go by the fear of falling down.

The answer is, 'No.'

The childhood bruises and pains, after falling down, were part of learning eventually marking our growth.

Similarly, as we grow up, we do fear the failures. The difference is childhood bruises, hurts and pains are just physical they remain out on the skin, though they may leave a scar behind but are not impacted much.

But as we grow, the falls and the failures we face, in our life impacts deep inside within our souls originating fears to over shadow our courage and confidence. We feel vulnerable to have those tremendous pressure and stressful life.

We feel the hurt and the scars are rooted deep within which prospers fears.

The fears to overcome the pain.

The fears to overcome the despaired life.

But with a little courage and positive outlook things can be changed. Things can be changed with choices we make.

Make a change. It just requires a start. Yes, the change is messy initially.

People talk about all the best they could ever and about my decision to take over the change.

But I was determined to get out of this.

I started opting changes, first shifting from a negative thinker to a positive thinker. We need to identify the strength that we possess as a signature that could be used as a base to build up a wall of confidence layer by layer thus demolishing our so called fears. And I could very well spend time in introspection and identify the missing elements that needed for me to start my walk. It started with my despair. I needed to walk somehow. Thus when I structured myself through serious introspection and self-awareness my past life lessons and experiences helped me to refocus on my present situation and I could now figure out solutions to my problems more succinctly and the roots of insecurity were visible.

I kept culminating hope and faith. After all, life is all about series of choices.

Seek the differences between negatives and positive shades of life. I do see inspiration in everything around that is the greatest gift that we are granted. Thus when I see the flames of fire raising high and low glowing yet sending a calm message. As the role of fire is to glow, give light and warmth.

Also we know the fact that the celebrations are witnessed around bonfire and grief around cremation fire. But in all the circumstances the role of fire is not moderated. It keeps glowing giving warmth and light. So is life, it has to glow, spread happiness, harmony around.

No life should die before it lives a life to the fullest. Life can't be dead or silent Life has to be very much "ALIVE."

With time, your greatest pain starts to heal and thus becomes your greatest strength, which can now cleave all the adamant walls.

Keep smiling – A living series

27
Mark Your Presence

Remember, what you tolerate would continue and what you resist would persist.

Both diverged paths need to be guarded as deep within us as only we know the best where we are compatible with and we do know in clarity which areas need to be worked upon like a mountain climber knows where his destination is every time he climbs forward. He looks at the peak and adapts more courage to finally reach over the top.

But what if he shifts his focus and he changes his mind, seeing the valley getting his mind flooding with fears.

What he will allow will surely continue even if he reaches somehow. He would feel nowhere to go as his will power is dominated by fear.

But if he had not allowed fears to keep streaming, he would have reached the top with confidence and positive approach and would had loved to seek new horizons and peaks that are yet to be explored.

So, whatsoever you choose, do focus giving your hundred percent and in doing it so you would explore yourself as a new individual, who has accomplished the task being determined and you are successful to mark your presence.

You should always have something to look forward that matters you the most. The most important or something that you're looking for as a hope to carry out your walk.

Look forward. When you're not striving any goals, you're allowing yourself to hold and slowly you get lethargic and decay and in this way the continuity of enthusiasm is been blocked

Of all the pits most dangerous is the pit, when we back fall devoid of self-confidence and low self-esteem, which precisely was conceived and dogged by own able hands as you allowed a block of fear.

I believe that when we are able to analyse our goals and are focused on that with determination, we truly lift our lives to our best performing potential.

You just need to highlight the areas of concern and erase your fears that are restraining you and that are holding you back and you are unable moving forward. Seeking the best solutions to your problems and passionately working towards purposes of your life mark your presence and be alive, don't just exist.

Let me illustrate a simple example here spotlighting the metaphors again.

Just imagine the energy every morning that predominantly marks its presence without fail. The sun never missed out his role.

Just feel the sumptuously drops of rains which never fail to fall downward quenching the thirst of earth never missing its focus delivering the best fullest rains which again marks its presence sufficiently making us believe in possibilities enthusiasm that dwells in the processes and events called life.

Just check out the sparkling lights of twinkling stars marking their presence in fact more prominent during darkest running show.

So, there's a largely displayed messaging content of universe's that keeps us redirecting to live our lives to our fullest potential and as similar as mustering our presence everyday here on earth.

Guard your time here on earth with possibility of life in enthusiasm, once the time evades, it will never show up again, once it is gone it never makes its appearance, marking its presence as well as yesterday today and tomorrow.

But remember, that you have to mark your presence and the opportunity is only today the very now.

So what are you waiting for?

Engage your time in strategically investing a little, for yourself articulating your commitments and focusing on your purposes.

The aspirations and your goals should be stretched further beyond your thinking. Always do remember that discipline is the key to every little goal that you want to accomplish. Just make it as a self-reminder, making it your habit. Discipline means inculcations of the habits that will move you closer to your achievements.

Abundance of will power and discipline can contribute to a fascinating performance.

Keep smiling – A living series

28

Master Your Path in Simplicity

I see simplicity reflected through happiness. Being simple elevates my inner peace. Here's my happiness that dwells. I feel comfortable with myself my life.

I admire my life when it's out of complexities. There's a tremendous power in this positive affirmative keywords that keep me going on and on and on...

Consistently, for very long, I did harbour thoughts of living in a perfect life, but I wasn't right. Life circumstances started playing havoc and I was surrounded by uncertainties. Times turned very hard, making me feel decay.

I started to die a little every time. I did experience harsh realities of life. Almost like change of people's behaviour that reflected their true colours and I could feel the negative influences that impacted me tremendously.

And, usually, people at this time just try to captivate us in their perceptions and try so, whatever it takes, to convert us into their mould and sculpt the image as they like, so we can accommodate the place in the frame that they have designed and expect us to adapt the world without any resistance or the same would be fortified as challenge for them.

No one cares as we die inside in the process. People try smothering the real of you in the process and just make you silent. Scrambling without any purpose, I was finding hard to cater all the negativity of life, while life unfolded same patterns day, night, months, and years. Slowly making me dead inside every time tears staining the pillow.

Times ripped me making me more confused and drained me completely leaving me empty, unable to even understand what I am supposed to do, emotions surfing up and I was on a unending trip, climbing a rough terrain and life was proceeding meaningless towards a long dark tunnel, I found myself entangled in a web of unknown fears, like a sprinkle of rebelliousness was overpowering me, but that's not accepted.

I learnt long before that it's very easy access for our thoughts, to be penetrative and slip into various forms of negativity. When I allow myself to be submerged in these life draining negative thoughts, I actually leave no room for gratitude.

I began to take everything for granted and consider life as an easy flow. All the love and consideration is often replaced with anger that adds frustrating behaviours at times that we are unknowingly enveloping into self-pity. But I started to understand the true reasons and the message hidden that was indeed the life was demanding for me to change.

Whereas, if I only allow positive thoughts to play the role, I would be successful to focus on good things in my life.

The point is to gear up your minds, gaining more attention to look up only positive and simple thoughts that refrains you from worrying about unmanageable circumstances.

I do strongly recommend that continuous efforts keeps you moving like easy flow of water, while not participating and fearing the unknown makes you paralysed.

Positive affirmations are the key to master a beautiful life. Being positive: Being Simple. Just play your role here.

And just submit yourself to god.

I did submit and surrender myself to god and I prayed,

"If you put me on this path, then lead me. I can't see the way nor do I have that strength."

Now, I see happiness is in simplicity. I find my inner peace when I participate in life's simple things; I get a chance to witness pleasure in simple achievements. I'm more confident now when I'm able to perceive simple strategies to the unbalancing thoughts.

I enjoy simple moments with my children and spending time with them, sharing all the day's events and happening. This just creates tremendous amount of positive energy leaving you enlightened from within. You're at peace from within now. This indirectly makes you strong. It's essential to count your blessings instead of dwelling in all that's never seen. I'm blessed with so many special people they are blessing in my life and they add happiness to my life.

I just avoid complex, daunting issues with simplicity by being in patience. My mission is to make every moment fulfilled in true life and worthy and more persistent towards keeping things simple.

So, how often you feel that life is simply beautiful and worth living?

Do you get clinched in between the place of boredom and complexities?

Do you ever ask yourself how you'll feel if you opt for a simple approach to life?

The answers to all the questions will highlight where your path is leading you.

Master your path, in simplicity being in patience and trusting your journey.

Make a change to cause a difference and challenge yourself to test your abilities that the difficulties are demanding from you. Yes, you are capable.

Keep smiling – A living series

29

No Storms are Forever

Raging storms, hardships of life, complex circumstances are just like redirected pages of life that resemble the most accredited way of lessons to be learnt. It also reflects the message - 'Yes, life tests us in many ways.'

If we want a change, we need to be accustomed to look out of the frame, be out of our comfort zones, and we need to stave off distractions that make our path hazy and blurry. And we should try to feed our goals of positive perceptions.

Times may be hard and the cause of despair may be many, which may cause us to lose all our hopes on life, unable to see what lies ahead and the horizon may look blur. Events could be devastating at times when you face loss of someone whom you love.

The sufferings may tend to have a more negative impact on your own self regardless of all your efforts making you give up and "I can't" may be the only thought that is left deep within you.

But I want to focus here on all those people, who learned deeply from all the trails, from the hardships and just walked in courage and grace. Those inspiring people who left their stories behind are to be saluted.

Martin Luther King was forced to surrender his seat and was forced to stand for next ninety miles. His words from the speech delivered

"I have a dream," became immensely famous. Later, he was also awarded the Noble prize in 1964. He fought for rights and became a leader of the American civil rights movement.

The Beatles were rejected by Decca records executive Dick Rowe. The Beatles were also rejected by Philips, and finally a contract was offered by subsidiary of EMI called Parlophone. George Martin, the producer, and this is how the most interesting and influenced band 'Rock n Roll' marked the page of the history.

We never know what future holds for us, if you feel life isn't going your way, don't despair and opt to give up as most of us just tend to give up very easily.

This is completely understandable that times break you.

But do we care that we have responsibilities, there are people who care for us.

We may be there only world…!

If depressing glimpses continues its impact on your life, then the fact appears prominent, resulting flashed suicidal tendencies and leaving you disappointed in extreme loneliness.

It's even more stressful, when these thoughts are bandaged deep within. It's like emptiness has invaded your soul.

So, just wake up and start talking on the serious subject for the discussion and start the bridge building concept. This is only possible if we look forward and try to see this out of frame in just a little positive way, exploring best from life.

This may be a wakeup call for you and, in fact, demand a change in life.

When we look towards a more optimistic view, we can suppress all those causes that were draining you towards emptiness, the pain of loss, the burdens of hopelessness are thus just pulled away resulting a renewal of you.

You try to reconsider your own choices which earlier you feared to opt for.

Thus, yes, we just need to overpower the negatives over positives and yes, it's POSSIBLE.

It is likely that you may even find someone very close whom you can share your experiences your pain, it's just you need to figure out more life alternatives which prosper positive feedback into your thoughts and revive the hope that you lost in your life.

Review the problems or hardships as just an evolution of your own self. Take this as a turning point of your life and not an end. Put all your efforts to build back the bridge back to your life which will be easier.

Try to recognise the confusion created by struggling times may be disturbing and it may break you, but a little more awareness into positive outlook may break the ice.

Darkness may be a significant call that may outshine as beginning of your life journey – just think about it.

Just not reacting to the things which we can't change, at the same time there's no need to keep standing and getting immobilised. The universe is never late to answer your calls.

Have you noticed flowing water? Just gaze the serenity and purity it redeems. And now, focus on a small pond which envelopes sometimes stagnant water, you can clearly observe the difference. Yes, you can now notice the difference.

Look at both the waters and just take a glance on both descriptions. Still water appears to be dark and hazy, the colour also changes, pungent smell etc...., water thus virtually loses its true identity.

Thus negatives atmosphere around you can suck your energies out of you, if you do not keep walking the walk of life.

Just remember… No storms are forever.

"To be yourself in a world that is constantly trying to make you something else is the greatest accomplishment."

– Ralph Waldo Emerson

Keep smiling – A living series

30

ON YOUR MARKS... GET SET GO

Refocus - Revive some more strength and run your race, Restructuring your goals...

"If there is something great in you, it will not appear on your first call. It will not appear and come to you easily, without any work or effort. "

– Ralph Waldo Emerson

You're a strong and a confident player, on this road of life. Do you take enough responsibility for making a difference to your own life? Do you spare some time analysing the life you want to see for yourself?

Indeed, everyone would like to see him or her as a great successful candidate for the role. It's yet, as simple as this, what you resist will continue until you faced with more of courage.

It's time to refocus and review the things that are not working. Make some important decisions right now to what's most important to you, in your life.

Well, it all requires a little amount of courage and a little pinch of discipline to be sprinkled, garnishing the platter of awesome life. We can't continue to live in fear of unknown and unseen tomorrow and keep stretching our lives much smaller than it's meant to be.

Dare, Desire, Dream, do it.

We have to be on the track, running our own race.

A choice has to be made now whether you are looking for a better version of you, refocusing the best way to get through the process. We have to set some goals when we do this as we know we are here with a purpose.

Goals help us to achieve what we're seeking. Goals redefine our purposes here.

Be yourself, set some real goals dwelling on the possibilities, affirming your key asset and that's your strong will power.

It's not that you're afraid to accept change or that you fear to face the real challenges.

It's just to keep simple and clear that propels you more closely to your success. On achieving small success, you feel happy and contented. You're able to finish what you started. You witness your purposes and missions to be accomplished are now much easier.

This roots your confidence and at this juncture, I truly recommend my favourite quote from, my book 'Elements of life' "On achieving small victories, double your will power."

We got to fight all the forces holding us back. Redirect all your energies into goal setting if you're seeking a magnificent transformation of self.

At the same time, we got to accept our mistakes and rectify them. When we do so, we clear all the unexplained clutter, making our life simpler and easy. It's said that by accepting our flaws we are a step closer towards our purposes and is yet another small accomplishment to be cherished. We are work in progress, we have to learn, accept, and grow at every stage of life.

Making some priorities, writing them down, working one by one, each time tracking the tiny flaws, rectifying them steadily but still pursuing the target with discipline and creating some guidelines can do wonders.

As you rise above, to choose a life that will make difference, you'll face the voices of disagreement.

But don't give up. Recognise the voices, take it as a compliment. Accept the criticism bravely. When we react to our critics, we give them full marks for their evaluation. So, just remain calm. We would strive hard to accept this and we do seek explanation we do engage fierce defence mechanism although the words have made the impact. We need to be comfortable with our silence and stillness as this would contribute making us a good listener.

Accept and walk further, don't let these words hold you back.

Don't forget that you're a strong warrior now; you're on your track and remember an elite performance can silent all the voices.

Noting the voices of critics as the mark of improvements that is to be keenly explored and worked upon, just walk ahead.

And once rectified, you're now stronger than yesterday to face all that's on the way. Run your race and rejoice your success immensely. So, what are you waiting for? On your marks, get set go…

One introspective quest is to define who are you; since lack of self-esteem is the root cause to many problems

Keep smiling – A living series

31
Opportunities Slip Away

At times, when nothing seemed to be working and I was entangled into the quest of unavoidable circumstances, I suffered lack of self-confidence.

'I need to stop and revive all the issues surfing up like a giant wheel.'

This reassurance was a spark to all the unanswered queries that I was trying to figure out. Instantly, my whole life started improving once I realized that everything hinged on the choices I made. In fact, what I learnt from my difficulties was that circumstances do highlight in our life, to flash how much we are already given and how much we are prepared to cater the unseen that's emerging right across the path.

I searched a simple meaning to the word 'change' and to seek the answer; I needed to start exploring the events, which were left behind on the last turn that I crossed. Yes, I immediately figured out the best answer and that was, the best word for a positive living diary. I frame it as an attitude that everyone should possess and the word is '*Start*.' So now, I have been able to write down a beautiful sentence in my personal journal.

"*To make a change, we need to start with a seed called desire.*"

When applied to the best of my own perception, I drew an affirmative conclusion regarding opportunities. We got to grow through them intentionally in positive perception recognizing the purposes and the cause.

As all opportunities come suddenly and slip away silently through the back doors. We have to be alert in recognizing them and allowing them to foster ourselves to the path of personal growth through vivid experiences.

Recognizing the opportunity, you get a chance to shine out with best options contrasting the best at same time, instead of wallowing the problems and not putting your best efforts limiting your achievements of life.

The responses that you make to the opportunities knocking around you thus help you to design the graph and calibre it to the mark of your own destinations. Sometimes, you desire to do something about your life and you start to weave the uneven threads somehow depicting the best way out.

And this desire happens to be the greatest turning point. Following the line are the thoughts, that when blended with a purpose, do converge the possibility of the dream come true.

You can now start the change and aim your success but if you fail to recognise the opportunities, you will be standing on the runway similar to the sea foam struggling against the rocky shores, waiting for tides to make the way.

When you are determined in pursuing your goals into actions, thus implementation of the same draws you closer to, achieving the deserving success that you are seeking. When you really desire something concrete to be the part of your life, and that which further needs to be re-organized, you're willing to stake all your future with one great cemented thought of 'self believe'

And now you're ready to turn the entire wheel of your destiny in your favour. These thoughts that converge with self believe and strong will powers are significant statements making the difference that you need for a change to be seeded.

And to make a change you need to start recognizing the opportunities knocking around the corner.

Apparently, your goal would not shape into the mould you perceive unless your setup is for a definite purpose and foster it with a progressive cause. But yes, constantly intensifying your desires into something that is very important can make you accredited for a change that is for you, by you, for your benefit and for your betterment. The important point of reminder here is that don't you dare to quit when temporary defeats overtake you.

Take it as a challenge and just keep walking, being committed to the cause with a power of harnessing self-discipline in every aspect of life. No one is spared here to experience a life which is hassle free no life is perfect and we all must face what is to be faced. Certainly the fact remains that you and I do possess an incredible power to make a choice and rise above all the circumstances that seems to be inevitable now. Thus we can rise and shine above all the life pressures gracefully. So, what's your strategy to pick the cards of opportunities that are playing tricky?

Be aware and be prepared to recognize the knocking opportunities as they often appear to come from very different directions to that we expect and also in a very different form.

That's the key card that they keep playing, making us confused, while slipping away from the back doors silently.

Efforts keep you moving forward, once stopped you are paralysed. We often choose the path that is easy and keep escaping to face the realm unaware of the fact we could have eliminated the fear by facing the truth and completing our task which we try so hard to avoid.

Keep smiling – A living series

32
Paint a New Picture

Being positive and taking responsibility has been an important element that I've opted thru my hardest time in life. And it's an essential driving force that keeps me going in all odds and has never wavered. What I feel is that problems and failures are to be looked at into a different way that reflects a brighter note as I agree that passing through them we can bring our unique self. There's no escape from the fact that these are part of our life without which there's no scope of improvements left.

Problems, failures, hardships actually strike our paths to make us more creative and polishing us to our brightest skills. Failures encourage us to work with more discipline and highlights the urge that we need to put some more sincere efforts to get desired results.

Have you ever tried to know why some of the people sail out smoothly in life, while some struggle throughout but never reach the destinations or achieve their goals? Most probably, the thin line which separates them is there approach and outlook towards life. The major concept here reflects is their thinking.

I believe that the place where you find the possibility is the 'new'-where the unknown resides, which is not yet explored and as we figure out the possibilities to overcome failures, all the pain that we feel shall eventually subside and a new, possibly, more determined, wiser and stronger of you will emerge.

Positive thinking often relates more about positive psychology and as the option to be more in acceptance of positive thoughts which dilutes most of the stress related issues. Let me mention more about the real meaning to the definition of positive thinking. Well, it's again all about your perception, the way you look or the way you understand the situation.

It's just as simple and similar to looking at life through very soft lenses like you admire a beautiful rose.

Yes, often we get tempted with the beauty of a rose, its colour, fragrance and this certainly has an excellent impact. Positive thinking tends to focus on affirmed status of the issues that are to be handled, being more practical. It further reflects inner monologues that enhance the attention to hear your inner voice, thus enabling you to ignore negative aspects while approaching the issues with a very clear positive mind-set and settled perceptive.

If you really want to change your life, you need to change your thoughts and all that requires is just a start, a beginning with you.

It could be a simple situation you're facing right now. Try to find out what if that could be used a medium of self-analysis and awareness.

Certainly, brooding over the problems only invite more of negative impacts. Some days back, I was the one who thought positive thinking is just a concept which holds true only in some books or movies. My life was in mess while still facing all the odds. I wondered every morning why did I deserve such an existence. But the circumstances were propelling up good enough to force me give up my trust on life. I had to finally decide as I figured out that life could get even worse. I started studying the concept of being positive more closely. I started with a small step of trying to ignore immediate decisions for the troubled issues. I stayed calm, trying my best to give time to myself. Positive thinking is not done overnight; it takes time. I began reading all I could find on being positive – Books, web, newspaper articles.

Some words do make an impact and that's what exactly happened. Sceptical at first, finally I got its influence overtaking all my sheltered concepts. I began with a new routine added in my stressed life and that was music.

I kept myself occupied with some soft music that helped me not only de-stress, but I could feel the changes.

I began to seek better options in all the problems that once were pretending that they would never get resolved. Using the positive concept as a tool, I started the change. I was looking for. Healing from a stressed life did not happen overnight and all of sudden. Yes, it took interminably long, but it happened.

I started instantly using a softer approach by taking time and not interfering in the natural flow of life. I overlooked all the negatives that could actually trigger again at an instance.

Instinctively, using best options for the problematic areas, I started to paint a new picture of my life. I began affirming brighter sides of life which now transformed me with a purpose of living more in enthusiasm.

So, do you envision your life struggling in the impacts of highs and lows? Do you feel yourself happy and contented?

Your answers will categorise where you fall…

A positive thinker or a negative!

You can transform your life.

You can make best of your life.

Paint a new picture for yourself.

It is never late to start a new life or to dream. You'll discover that once you begin to transform, your life starts to change, making you feel happy. And you meet a new you, who has a bright and improved outlook towards life. There are small changes initially, but these are the doorways towards the transitions which lead a larger change that is waiting to embrace you. Enlightened within, positive mind and many such vast capabilities do exist in all of us. We just need to make a small effort to harness the potential we have, thus we are able to make a change, we are looking for, and hence achieving the goals in spite all the odds.

Just make a start. Make a better choice. Paint a new picture of life.

Clinging to the fears is just making yourself imprisoned to the circumstances. The entire result lies to the choices we make so whether we opt the path of greater or less resistance doesn't matter much since both have stored something valuable in the form of life experience.

Keep smiling – A living series

33
A Place for Me

"Men seek retreats for themselves: houses in the country, seashores and mountains; and thou too art won't to desire such things very much," said Marcus Aurelius.

It's very important to self-analyse and be in calmness at times, opting to be in solitude to reenergize and for harnessing your potentials for leveraging your inner beliefs. Each and every one does long for happiness and peace at the end of the day. We constantly look out for a place to be in solitude and seek a quiet room inside our own self like the depth of calm oceans that are never touched however the rough waves surfacing onto it. Thus, we need to create a quiet room within our mind that can serve as relaxing chamber at times of emotional turmoil. I understand that it's not easy but we need to constantly search this quiet place and retreat it with quietness over and over that we do so much possess. We can always manifest to what we believe we can thus with our persistence build a quiet room in our mind, which can act as our own decompression unit that can help you distress refreshing you to work more efficiently in your life. A place for yourself that can reconnect you back to this beautiful life, rejuvenating your presence as an extension card.

Do make your working area your living room a beautiful place that can add peaceful and tranquillity with some flowers and best draperies adding a sprinkle with mild room fresheners. Always let the fresh air keep flowing in instead of the compact gloomy rooms, so whether its home or your workplace make sure you get to see some nature everyday with windows open for fresh air to embrace your skin a refreshing tone always rejuvenating you every minute. Let the colours of the wall be from mild cool and calm textures that soothe your eyes with good and less furniture and no distracting elements of negativity; quite simply a beauty of calmness that makes everything splendour.

As we all are aware and we witness inner disturbances that does play an opposite role of tranquillity, which is the outcome of either immediate response perhaps more specifically when we are too sensitive and we are over responsive to any of the surfaced issues. The best remedy at this juncture is to build a thin lining or a soft wall between the disturbing elements and you by merely adding a little factor of delay or by not responding immediately.

Thus, this way we trigger our relaxation stimuli in spite of disturbing situations, we can always practice it daily, making it a habit as it serves as the best remedy in many of the burning issues. Hence, we neutralise our stubborn habits of being quick responsive or over responsive and we give time to our thought process to seek the best solutions to the issues. So, when we venture in our quiet room, we now experience that we have enough space to get everything work in our favours with relaxation practices. Dedicate yourself to transforming your inner self.

Culture your discipline into whatever you're pursuing as achieving small victories will double your willpower. When our will power gets escalated, we perform to our best abilities.

If at all you need to set boundaries, set some priorities - make a list of dos and don'ts.

The best way to reconnect with yourself is through meditation. Practice closing your eyes for five minutes every day, focusing on your breath, gazing into your inner compass for more clarity. Being in peace initiates practice of being in patience too, the key to most of the trouble making issues in today's stressful life. Being cheerful, being at peace, being calm is always an extremely

significant way to enhance your mood and well-being. Remember that the excuses you make to yourself are nothing but your fears about the results or the outcomes. And I do personally believe there's no meaning in negative assumptions unless we participate and give our best.

Read good books. Books are treasures of wisdom and words of great people, who share their journey their experiences.

Go for some long walks any time of the day as per your convenience but make sure it's a disciplined routine that can reconnect you to be with you for some more time there's no use you meet your friends midway again gossiping and gathering back the emotional clutter. Practice deep breathing. Connect spiritually. Breed as many positive thoughts...

Use positive affirmation. When you find yourself emotionally and physically fit, you start loving and living more, boosting your self-esteem. You experience the joy of achievement in small accomplishments.

Care about how many people you can help than how much appreciation you receive. Understanding that the excuses you make are nothing more than the fears will help. Do what make you really happy. And remember that if something was hard to accomplish yesterday, it doesn't mean it will not be easy to do today.

Spend time in solitude daily as this will take you closer to yourself and that will make a drastic difference. You'll face the voices of disagreement though but still I insist being alone for some time with yourself works impeccably. Spending time alone will help you build your confidence. It will allow you to refuel the strengths that you need towards your vision for your goals.

Focus on living a healthy life style. Include lots of vegetables and fruits in your diet in such a way that all the requirements of protein and vitamins are supplied to the body. Drink plenty of water to cleanse and regulate the body-water balance, also detoxifying the body.

Hope makes us to move when we are confused to walk.

Keep smiling – A living series

34
Purpose Achievement

The centre line to any visionary and great ideas is purposes and positive thoughts. Whatever may be the goals but one should be focused with a purpose and determined to accomplish whatsoever is started.

It's important to walk the life with a purpose and more importantly is to work hard to attain that purpose, thus beginning to think about the real meaning to your life.

When we think on these terms we are able to recognise failure as a path to attain the purposes. We are able to make all conditions work in our favour. We are able to attempt every task more fearlessly and thus accomplishing the purposes. Achieving purposes is a path that keeps you going every time you feel like giving up. Purposes keep you moving in life and you're able to look forward with hopes. And, apparently, we do try our best in every field of life to do our best.

Once purpose of life is understood, we should be confident and focussed on achieving the same. Overcoming the doubts and crossing all fears just walk relentlessly in strong positive thoughts. If we allow fears to creep in, we are surely losing our sight. We are unable to move a step further, as we are now entangled in webs of uncertainty and doubts.

It's all the play of again determined mind-set and the will to overcome all the barriers which try to hook you in same place without any results. It's hence important to conquer your doubts and fears thus empowering the success over failures.

Now, your positive thoughts are allied with enthusiasm and you're willing to face all that's difficult. Now, you see your thoughts grasping the roots, adapting itself as a creative force towards more progressive growth and you're entitled for a sweet reap of the hard efforts you made, isn't it?

Now, you're looking more confident and determined, rather than a mere weak person, who is just brimmed in doubts and wavering thoughts.

Now, you're looking towards life with clarity and a vision.

Now, you know where the life is taking you, what are the flaws that are needed to be rectified? Now, you can figure out places that need to be refocused and be ready like a welder to smoulder the negative impact of thoughts on the mind and body. The thought factors play a vital role in the progress of life. Thoughts impact the graph of purposes and achievements.

So, what's your strategy towards pursuing your achievements?

Do revive the process and set some personal goals and purposes of your life. Once you set some personal goal you step in the arena which enables you to see all that was invisible and impossible once now so much sustainable and achievable.

Well, life would still surface up with uncertainties but being focused on your purposes would root a confidence in you.

You will now navigate through all the storms skilfully being positive.

The result will be that life will be filled with joy of achievement and success and a sense of happiness that you may fail even to realize that could be possible to experience.

Be honest with yourself and find clarity in your purposes.

Keep smiling – A living series

35
Reflections

Circumstances highlight how much you've already given in to life as a responsible participant.

I can relate that the experiences in my life that were to explore me.

I am grateful for all the circumstances that led me to know my inner self.

Fortunately, when I was in life's most vulnerable crisis, I was able to keep balancing through most of the inner turmoil under control. I'd promised no matter what I would never express my pain around my kids. Every day, I strived hard to find ways to keep away from all negative emotional waves while caring for them. After all, that was a tough time and I was determined to do whatsoever it took to just create a positive atmosphere.

No amount of positive thinking can replace you if you're not sure of yourself.

Remember 'Who you are.' Believe in yourself; that's the root. It's a procedure to refocus on yourself and finding your uniqueness. This enhances the best way to create a strong sense of self directions. You start making powerful decision switching to say a 'No' to what that makes you uncomfortable.

At times, when negative thoughts entangled me, I kept surfing the emotional waves that ripped me off. We do often face dilemmas sometimes unsure what will be the next move. Let me put more colloquially- have you been stuck in dire situations? That's the most surprising package of life's equations. Reoccurrence of uncertainties around you makes you more vulnerable thus anchoring you alone at the shore of negative influences. You start losing interest in life over- saturated with dark fears; your enthusiasm fades away eventually, forcing you to be deeply unhappy.

Suffering escalates more if you're surrounded by negative people. They try to capsize you in their frames. They want you to believe and perceive their perceptions. This makes you to surrender deep in depressions, thus leaving no scopes of evolution.

You got to find out the root. No amount of positive thinking or affirmations would help if you don't focus on your unique self.

You need to create a strong self-esteem first.

Remember, who you are. Self-belief is the root that you're trying to explore and indeed you're not seeing this clearly now as your focuses are blurred since you're diving in darkness recording only failure and fears.

Don't give yourself hard time if you're not sure or fixed in uncertainties and there is no denial to the fact that when adversities strike, your life is battling a hard time to make a balance. And the best thing to do is asking yourself how you can make a balance with all the available possibilities, although it may be different from that you are expecting but still it may work for you.

When we are dissatisfied or disappointed with ourselves, how are we supposed to evaluate ourselves for a better performance?

When we hold low opinion of ourselves or we live in a more pessimistic outlook, we are sure to face unexpected results. Being low, you feel very hard to explain and express yourself. You won't be able to achieve opportunities and results that you are aiming for. You will find yourself heading down in course of life. But to move ahead, we need to see up we can't see back or see downwards, we are sure to face accidents. As in all the circumstances in life, our perception plays an important role and this factor decides the quality of life that we would be leading. You may make a choice to perceive your life as a victim with no escape, or you may make a choice to accept the facts and take it as a gate pass to your bright future.

Let your life project a new horizon that redirects you to see high skies of amazing opportunities and happiness. Replace all negatives with positives with self-belief and determined mind set, repeating it constantly and persevere. Learn to say 'Yes' to life. Implicate your views, your imagination and just simply believe that '*You can do it.*'

At my lowest, I found that I did lacked self-confidence. Trying hard to be out of my shell, I learned everything hinged on my choices and self believe.

In today's fiercely competitive life, fears of failures, stress do resonate constantly grooming out every possible problem.

You may feel life grounded to a halt. This negative attachment is not a mental illness, but yes incredibly saturated situation of life. Negative assumptions are just like another amazingly debilitating condition that develops instantly sometimes and hence needs to be rectified and should be attended immediately.

But with self-awareness, self believe and positive outlook, life can be progressive.

Whole life started to improve once the root cause was discovered. What I believe is that courage and confidence are just like habits and anyone can culture it for a beautiful life to be explored and experienced.

To make a change, we need to desire and initiate it.

Happiness and positive life are indeed very essential ingredients and are reflected as life learning threads embedded as everybody's journey.

No one is perfect. It's okay to be a little different if that makes you entitled to who you are.

Keep smiling – A living series.

36

The Ripple Effect: Making an Impact

Writing my positive words for life made me feel more comfortable with the best teaching philosophy of life.

Till day, I haven't yet opted more suitable tools for changes in the life more effectively than spreading across positive messages. Spreading positive words do result in one of the best rippling effect.

I feel glad when I get replies like

"You made my day," usually weekends, I make sure to put across some positive messages to my friends. And to inspire my readers here's the affirmations that would make the rippling impact.

This quality of your patience that you practice amazes me and let me draw your attention to the fact that these act of your adapting patience as a key calibre your performance as elite. You stand out from others in every aspect I'm inspired, as I witness your relentless devotion and hard work figuring out the purposes, that makes the path more successful towards attainment

Today is the day and it will shine in brilliance if you allow it to be. Sun or no sun doesn't allow anyone else to block the rays of happiness from reaching towards you. You can, if you believe. You can, if you desire. You can, if you acquire the strength to conquer your quest of unsettled thoughts. Don't allow the pain or the past situation to be so intense, that it captivates you to walk further that indirectly leads you to self-destruction.

After breathing toxins from the negative people or situations don't forget to exhale and remove yourself from the entangled environment. You can if you believe it's not hard, it's the mind-set that drives you towards success or failures. Look behind, that's the place you'll find your lessons that highlight and redirect you not to repeat the same mistakes.

Remember you've had the ability always and shall always be with you to make a change by opting a chance to take a great decision.

But yes, sometimes you have to be very clear in your mind.

Think before you take a critical decision making. If you make a wrong choice, the ability to do so again may be taken away from you. Be a positive example, it requires a great deal of courage to ignite a spark of change. Remember there falls a shadow between conception and creation. Be active take the responsibility work for the things that you believe.

If you want to leave your footprints on the sand, don't drag your feet in confusion. It's always best to walk slow in confidence, rather than running aimlessly.

Shores often tell their stories of the feet that walked on them, of the waves that touched to leave an impression that relay an inspiration to those who are still fighting back to cross the stormy oceans.

In difficult times just be patience and remember some things in life are not to meant and are best to not have. Remember that life is a collage of courage, willpower, discipline just erases your fears and look beyond this philosophy can be stated more succinctly.

True enlightened people are those who experience happiness in small achievements and experience happiness on daily basis, tackling their weaknesses and fears much ahead, even if they have to dive deep into the unknown reasons or measures of discomforts they actively participate, resolving to live and improvise every aspect of themselves continuously.

Applied correctly life moves into the realm of ordinary to the excellence in shape of extraordinary, with your own effective and purposeful efforts.

I must alert you if you lack in willpower or decision making that's a weakness and if you're drifting still in the odds it's high time to make priorities in life and stamp out this ill habits immediately and you'll find;

No hurdles are too high for you to overcome and no challenge is too tough for you to surmount.

Rise with the rising sun and let it bless you in abundance of energy.

At times despair and hopelessness is all that's left around, and you will face a certain period of life to be the most dreadful.

Since the most hurting experiences come from all the people we had trusted the most.

When you will brood over how you'll face the world out there.

When our self-esteem and dignity is wounded, we are broken and shattered into pieces and suffer inside.

It demands a great deal of courage to make a change and trust yourself. You start making strategies which define you to be a winner: you talk like a true winner. But certainly if you're not strong from within and try to compromise with the situations; you will reflect a defeat in your eyes and can become an easy prey for the outer world once again.

I do understand you're stressed I'm just trying to intersect the chain of stressed thoughts that make you worry so much. Be positive. Be strong.

I appreciate your efforts.

You've been through extremely bizarre conditions and circumstances and I do respect you for all. Believe me you've the tenacity and determination of which you're not fully aware.

Just think for a moment about all the obstacles that you've successfully managed to overcome in the past.

You can walk further. You're strong. And I really appreciate you.

Be positive. I'm sure soon there's a way out and all the delayed issues will be dusted off.

Don't just stress and curb your enthusiasm towards life. I know you are on a right path for a quantum leap forward.

I appreciate your efforts and admire you. Just be positive. Dusty roads have unclear vision. Let the wind blow carry away the dust. Relax don't think much and occupy yourself in something more fruitful like simply go for a walk and after few hours calmly sort out the poised issues.

The fact is life has never given you anything for free, now you have to allow yourself to strongly rely on your abilities.

Once you're aware of your strength each troubled issue will be within your reach. Be calm be positive and you'll be able to turn every initiative into success. You'll see you gaining trust in life again and rediscovering passion as never before thus you make a forward leap. It's quite obvious that everything you've ever dreamed of and that you desire will often show up in different package than you envisioned. So be strong and accept the things that you can and change the one that you can't.

There's absolutely no problem to break down the resistance of those who want to curb your enthusiasm towards life as your heart knows that you're right and on the right path.

Connecting back enthusiastically with life in every moment.

And lead bravely. Do that, and the future is yours!

Whatever you choose, make it work more efficiently.

These simple acts of kindness make you learn and grow truly being human.

Keep smiling – A living series

37
Submissions

Life journey requires a balance of acceptance, letting go and move on spirit.

Sometimes, dark phase of lives often referred as to be the most difficult phase has to be concluded, so just keep walking. Move ahead persistently towards whatsoever life has stored submitting ourselves resigning to whatsoever is holding you back from moving on forward in life or in giving up, surrendering, changing and accepting the life.

Some of the great philosophy quotes inspiring quotes that makes a statement of life. We cannot step into same river twice. We can always look forward to life by considering our little flaws and mistakes as lessons that are important learnt instead of feeling low and adapting to the sense of setbacks or considering ourselves inferior. Instead, we can attain more wisdom and strength adding this as a life experiences and boosting our self-confidence.

It's all the play of how we submit ourselves to this great assessment of life.

Yes, we do get disturbed facing rejections by others at times, but the fact remains that it doesn't mean you don't deserve a second chance. Just take it as a progressive criticism which helps you to explore and learn more. We see celebrities and world leaders criticized for being on a different path.

Remember, to walk on righteous path is never easy. Never get influenced by the criticism or negative feedbacks take it as a compliment that you were assessed in a right manner.

How many times do we accept our flaws? Do we take enough efforts to rectify? So, why not accept the comments of critics and work more effectively.

And at one point, you'll find most vulnerable when people would judge you. Strange paradox though, many of the judgement will come from those whom you know very well and those who don't even know how you travelled your journey.

You will scan your eyes around to seeking a shoulder but you won't find one. Yes, everyone needs comfort and support at those times. Never lose yourself at this juncture, no matter what and no matter how much you are accused- just don't give up.

In fact, this is the right time to stand erect and walk straight and show you're strong in and out and who doesn't get influenced by the temporarily surfaced stressful factors.

Never let yourself down as these are the times when you are being tested for your ability to surface up the waves or just flow along the waves. When you're tested, how effortlessly you stand on your ground because you know you can trust yourself. And never forget that you're never alone. God himself will hold your hands and help you to cross these seasons of uncertainty and hardships.

God loves you and he never fails to see you ever even if everyone around you were successful to do so.

God believes in you and is always walking along by your side all the time.

1. You can live in past or long for a bright future.

2. If you don't change for the better, you may be at the edge of extinction.
3. What can be more challenging than to challenge you to improve?
4. Confidence re-conditions all the unbalanced barriers and elevates your purpose of living more significantly.
5. Abundance of willpower and discipline can contribute fascinating performance.
6. The tougher the challenges, the better lessons inculcated.
7. Changes are for better, for growth and when you accept a change in positivity, it starts a new beginning.
8. Peace of mind is when we are able to live in the present moment more focused and more in enthusiasm.
9. Ultimately, the destiny unfolds according to what we choose in our lives.
10. Life is: The collage of vibrant lessons, enveloped as experiences.
11. Lessons are to be mastered as self-learning teaching aids.
12. Courage gives us self-control to perform constantly.
13. The degree of your determination makes the purpose of life more meaningful and possible.
14. The responsibility to make a change lies in you.
15. We feel happy when all is perfect, but tiny little change creates a complexity in our thoughts at once.

    We are dissatisfied often either -if pleasure doesn't last or if pain doesn't vanish.

16. We will remain unhappy if we deliberately interfere in natural flow of life experiences.
17. It's always hardship and struggles that brings out best qualities of you.
18. Many of us don't take enough responsibility for the magnificent event called life. We make it toxic with self-created anxieties and worries.
19. We trade our lives collecting achievements not aware that these are external rewards for investment of our precious life.
20. Struggling in negatives, we are actually webbing our inner selves, restraining growth of life and happiness.
21. Complexity can be cut back. We can make choices for a simpler life. Needs versus wants can be focused and limited.
    1. Goals ~ Goals help us to achieve our purposes.
    2. Challenges ~ Challenges are nothing, but our test to check out our abilities, to withstand all the unavoidable circumstances and demand a check on personal responsibility.
    3. Drive ~ The best way to drive life is from inside just like an automobile, keeping balance of mind, using your skills in patience.
    4. What's being positive? It's an act to response to a problem with confidence, ruling out negative influences.

Keep smiling – A living series

38

Success Walks In

You're entitled to great success when you are not paralysed by the defeats and the unavoidable, inevitable circumstances on the way as you didn't hold yourself much into agonising over what you didn't achieve but you made certain improvements. You opted for self-awareness, you started exploring your hidden potentials, you managed to craft your skills, and you kept being devoted.

You logged some discipline and time management in your journal.

With all your self-belief, efforts, positive perceptions, consistency and courage, ruling the hard work, you were successful and did managed to finish what you began.

Success would never come to those who engage themselves in all the time comparing with others and want to lead someone else's life.

But success would definitely knock the doors, who ask for a change, who accept the challenges on the path with a ray of hope and keep their faith working in positive directions no matter what. Success leads the path, walking in front to those who seek, who remain strong and focused and to those who redeem the positive thoughts that they would do the best.

Although, you ignored all the traps, all the attractions and illusions on the way, you made some huge sacrifices, you crossed over the roughest terrains with your enthusiasm, the difficulties waned off springing you bright.

Just always remember:

Success is not overnight; it's the outcome of years of your hard work, devotion and sacrifices you have made on your way.

You have to submit and surrender, hence winning the war of difficulties with courage and patience.

You're accredited by true a success. You're a true winner now because that's the true success and not accumulating the powers and filling your coffers with gold.

The path to success is the hardest and the longest one: -

You can't pick the fruit when it's green; you got to wait for a golden harvest with patience. You got to encourage yourself to be in patience and in hope for the time of harvest may get delayed sometime.

All you got to do is just sow a seed of self believe and respect the time between the sowing and harvesting in patience and in faith.

The transformation would be amazing and you'll be profoundly filled with a new energy to meet a new yourself when you would excavate the one, who dwelled inside you, was occupied with great powers and had enormous abilities to craft a new of you.

Remember, anything you want to be, you can, if your goals are clear enough with discipline and you're focused with a clear mind-set.

You have the potential to create a unique self, implementing the best of you, beginning right now because you're combed with courage and conviction. Only weak fail to climb the wall of success.

Keep smiling – A living series

39
Teaming up with Possibilities

The worst part of struggling times is the time itself. Here the complications that we encounter are that we are not sure of ourselves. We just focus on the surfaced issue, thinking more negatives rather than thinking about the perfect solutions and we try to finish as much as everything soon.

The implication of this result is that we just make a progress in millimetres in multiple directions.

Recognize:- what is essential.

Eliminate:- that is not required at all.

Collectively:- work into one direction for a steady progress.

If at all you find yourself surrounded by complexities, just pause for a moment and ask yourself "is this important thing right now that I could be doing" and if answer is "No," just stop.

Get out of the place for some time and engage yourself in some activity. Remember that your brain would recognise the signals in form of the thoughts that you breed. We can train our thinking into more creative and balanced way. Just we need to refocus onto our goals as we can work into goal setting and end results. As you breed a thought of goal setting automatically we start depending on our brain guidance system that helps us to achieve and thus we can feed to our conscious thoughts walking in believing in self and dwelling in possibilities.

Conversely, if we dwell in negativity, we continuously breed an image of failure so vivid that we could feel the consequences long before the action was accomplished. This does happen because being negative, we do evoke self-destruction in terms of confidence and yes, we do lack self-esteem as we are unsure about everything successively. Thus, when we dwell in possibilities we do add a winning feeling into our subconscious mind hence the desires to create and achieve what that we proposed becomes sustainable.

Well, this is not so difficult neither unachievable as it may reflect at the initial stages. But a little awareness and a shift of perspective would activate your mechanism to dwell and team up with possibilities. Let me add a simple example -we very often this mistake our daily life and we get flooded with thoughts and keep worrying about our future which results nothing but a new package of anxiety, stress, inadequacy is delivered with a feeling of giving up, thus we picture a failure well in advance that's not at all needed.

Adding to the fact the very important thought is that our brains cannot differentiate between a real failure and imagined failure, thus we exercise our muscles to break down temporarily for some time when we vividly imagine a negative thought and failures well in advance. When we do think in possibilities our brain does experience a feeling of victory and thus, we set our inner mechanism for achieving the success that we desire. Just create a thought of possibility in focus with a determined and focused view. Then, add up a vivid feeling that you would feel when the goals that are set would be accomplished more in clarity thus you empower your guidance system that's your brain and subconscious mind to work with achievable thoughts the internal mechanism is now geared up to guide you to take most important decisions helping you with more creative ideas and whatsoever that is needed to accomplish your goals.

Act in strength and in positive hope whenever you face difficult times perhaps when you are unable to decide what's the next move of life the situation is as similar to that we know we have to climb the staircase as we know the only way to reach top floor is via the staircase in case the elevators aren't working. We can't see ahead how many more stairs we have to climb, yet we do reroute the available option because the main focus remains to reach the destination, no matter how many hurdles and obstacles we face on our way. Yes, at times, we feel broken facing failures and tormented setbacks which do add depression, yet I recommend that at these critical times, redirect your mind to live in present in possibilities and in probabilities.

Act in strength while facing critical times and by acquiring the same positive approach now, move step-by-step ahead and in affirmations. See the courage you acquire to conquer all your fears getting faded away as it's just the impact of teaming up with possibilities the immensely powered positive approach inculcated by you and for you, work for you. Therefore, never treat any troubling issues or the hard times as a snag, instead, look it as an assignment that has to be accomplished. This is the age of distractions, setbacks at the workplace; lives overloaded with so much internet social networking, cell phones, and stressed lives competitions getting tougher every day at every level. Hence, it's very essential to put aside a little time for personal growth clearing the decks getting away with all the time available with us in some meaningful life. Most of us complain and whine about our problems. We can restore them instead, by using time in our favour. Remember, life is always in progress.

Perhaps, now, when you team up with possibilities you will find all the new opportunities ahead you just need to adapt some more courage and strengthen yourself to endure the most difficult situations. Adapt some more courage and defy the daily grind that weighs you down making you feel vulnerable.

Focus on what you want, what you are passionate about, discarding all the negative influences and the energy drainers look ahead by infusing a little more courage into your life.

The challenges that you have met are behind you and still you have to face what's stored for tomorrow. As the day departs, some of us do miss opportunities and some of us are down due to failures but remember that 90% of failures are not because people were defeated, it's because people were unsuccessful to walk long and got tempted by the temporary obstacles that were good enough for them to give up and yes they quit reaching very close to the destinations unaware of the facts that they could have achieved with a little more of patience.

When you redeem more of your self-belief, more of your courage, you flow significantly more like that clarity that we observe in ripples of water. Every champion was once a contender as no one is born as a leader or as an artist. They keep working hard and refuse to give up. Every setback is a blessing that signifies that something better is in store for you.

Keep smiling – A living series

40

THERE ARE NO QUICK FIXES

It's essential to maintain a discipline and gain a sense of self efficiency, everyday working a little bit harder.

When you see yourself overpowering all the fears and mastering the skills of self-discipline and self-confidence, you gain access to the highest legacies of self-esteem that's unshakeable. This enables the roots of self believe go deeper making you to excel the areas you're working achieving the goals that you're perusing.

Some people believe that self-confidence can be built and gain the best accreditation with some quick fixes of positive tools Yes, but a clear and distinctive outlined disciplinary approach is eloquent and with some self-competence every day, you overcome all the barriers.

Quick fixes never give long term solutions; it's just like a temporary relief. What is achievable more readily is being confident about you Now, take all the issues one by one working on it a little hard stretching the edges every time.

You can, you should and you're capable of being focused and determined while catering the issues that are to be solved. Set out and get ready for your journey of self-awareness. One should be confident of self-looking the past and analysing all that you've achieved so far.

This acts like encouraging fuel building confidence more concrete. Add some discipline every time. It's not hard to change ourselves quickly even if entangled in your schedules that aren't allowing you to look out for anything else. Believe me, it works a little discipline a little effort a little change in daily activities does get transformed in magnificent results.

Keep maintaining a daily stock of your life activities and where you're going in life. Just see back through your journey of life to see how far you have survived most difficulties, how far you've reached, how much more effort needed, what's the more relevant factor needed?

Do sincerely adapt to sacrifice a little for the target you're aiming to reach. There's no way to quick fixes or some way to shortcuts that display quick solutions to your problems.

It's just a successive journey starting with a self-belief, desire, determination efforts, sacrifices, confidence and yes, indeed, your knowledge and skills that you possess, anything that's lacking can be always figured out and worked out.

When we pass out under pressures of life gracefully that is when we are emerged as a great individual who can deal with life at any given time and this beautiful quality of you would inspire others and reflect beyond any comparison. It would engross your individuality as a winner of every situation allowing you to carve out a spectacular life that would indeed make you feel happy and proud of yourself. Commitment plays vital here; be sincere towards yourself. Focus on all the basics. Leverage your resources set some small goals and cherish them when achieved. Add a brick of self-confidence and start your journey now, accelerating towards your dreams.

Keep smiling – A living series

41

Times Change

I had made up my mind to stop crawling and take up a straight walk and self-publishing was one of my learning experiences.

As the thought for getting my book published percolated in my brain and also, there comes a time in life where we give up addressing flaws we can't correct and overlook blemishes we can't wipe clean and we start focusing, building strength, thus accentuating our positive hidden potentials.

Yes, I tried opting for traditional publishing and waited for some few months but eventually started tracking self-publishing options and this is how my debut book was launched and I opted for better options.

When we are no longer in a position to change a situation or we can't accept the unavoidable circumstances, we are challenged to bring a change in ourselves. Since I do believe that when we argue with reality, we are bound to suffer.

So, times taught me the best project to work is to work on ourselves and bring out best of our potentials and crafting your unique self. We got to work more in progressive positively filled options for the better change that we are seeking.

If we do not hope, we will never understand what opportunities were lying beyond our hopes. We have to unlock all the doors that open for us during times of adversities. We need to be patient and look for the opportunities that craft a new chance for our life, preparing us for a better time.

Times Change…

We all know there are some tiny little disciplinary rules of life, but somehow we tend to forget about it down the road.

Emotions are not our weaknesses but our strength and life is not about losing or winning but probably giving your best.

As I passed through the giant gates of the court through the back road, the heat was burning my head. Undaunted, I refused to take the front gate without any particular reason.

This ordeal had been going in from past more than two years now and I was acquainted with the entire site of the court by now. Through the back entrance was a temple where mostly everyone including the lawyers, reputed juries, criminals in chain, bowed their head to seek a peaceful hearing obviously in their favour in respective cases. I also used to have a glance and pray- "please take care of me."

That day was the judgement day as I climbed the stairs to first floor of family court. My tears not visible to the world while my heart was bleeding. Waiting for my call, I recollected all times good, bad, painful and devastating, but heard "now all is over…."

And I did not regret as I tried to keep things working more than two decades. The moment was tremendously hard to face when finally, the judge asked "Can anything be done still, are you sure you want to dissolve this marriage?" I said, "Yes, I'm sure. I want to dissolve this marriage as things aren't working out anymore … and I tried my best… past two decades."

I saw the judge in tears… I remembered my kids and signed the petition filed for the appeal while later the judge passed the divorce decree. Thus, I know that the walk of life is hard and to reach the apex in hardships is hard…

I've been through hard times, through valleys, and roads of stumbling rocks… Believe me, all seasons are never forever. All the troubles are never forecast for ever. Some times of life are encapsulated in pyres of suffering but this brings out the best of you. The price of anything is the amount of life we exchange for it.

We just need to refocus a little more and start starving distractions. We need to sacrifice, we need to be away from those who belittle your ambition and who bring you down emotionally.

While we wait ourselves for a better tomorrow, we do know somewhere in the corner of the heart that yes, things will be better. We get disappointed sometimes when realities do not match up to our expectations.

But we know that life has the tendency to spark some moments filled miraculously that do all the wonders needed to realize that.

At the end of the day while washing few dishes and turning off the lights alone with my thoughts, I realised that all that happens has a reason and with a grateful heart I know there's a positive light beyond the darkest hours of night…

And you might be the only one who is left in the whole world who believes in yourself… But that's all that is needed at the end of the day.

Keep smiling – A living series

42

TODAY IS THE DAY

Some people wait for stars to align, so many wait for a perfect day and so many waiting for a brighter day and for the time to be right.

While not everyone may hit similar threads, indeed they leap forward making a beautiful resolution.

Today is the day to avoid complex and daunting circumstances with a simple positive thought of self-belief.

I don't believe in tomorrow that hasn't yet arrived.

What we have is now.

But don't forget that we are all full of possibilities and surely dwelling with some unique qualities within us that need to be explored and crafted.

Yes, we stumble across unavoidable situations and certain issues occasionally, but those times do not last forever.

If you just think you want to cross the river standing on the shores, you won't be able unless you dive into the waters with self-belief. Similarly, situations or circumstance can't be dealt unless faced. We are not here to fritter our precious time when we have all the potentials to opt for best choices to be made on the way to make a difference and to make a change.

You're not supposed to wait for a perfect day to arrive. You've got all the ability and the responsibility to make the change that lies in you. Make a positive affirmation today and stand out. Make some beautiful resolution now. You have to throw all the shackles of your doubt and start believing in yourself now.

Make a change to cause a difference and challenge yourself to test your abilities that the difficulties are demanding from you.

Yes, you're capable. The moment you decide that you're not going to hold back yourself into the fears that are no longer serving any growth, you raise your life at that very instant and you're changed for a meaningful purpose of your life. You set the course of your own destinations, advancing in courage to make all the attempts walking courageously into the directions of your dreams accomplishing the resolutions you made.

You mark an excellent and important improvement in your journal and just stop worrying about the potholes on the road; just keep walking. Today is the day when you can make an attempt seeking the changes and achieving your targets and making your life worth living.

I firmly believe in the power of words that beautifully impact and play the role.

The words to inspire, the words in form of small affirmation and in prayers thus words do wonder. Simple affirmation makes me feel better and happy. Now, I see my life free of complex issues as I'm more tuned into finding happiness in simplicity. I'm more creative and confident now.

You're a person who dwells in possibilities; you're having all the courage and it is only the weak who will hesitate to climb the rockiest mountain.

But once you climb up high, you will find still more horizons to be explored. Just think about the current obstacles that are prohibiting you to attain your dreams. You have to overcome all your fears and cross all the roadblocks, to acquire the state of bliss that you so much deserve.

Once you recognize the obstacles and develop great passion and will power to overcome those stumbling rocks, you will witness amazing results and everything that was once impossible will get easy and be accomplished, leading you to the right place and making you a stand out in every situation of life.

Anything that you are seeking, you can get if your goals are clear and you're true to yourself in making the commitment. Positive words of affirmation to self-play a tremendous role.

Discipline, willpower and self-belief are the keys to unlock all the codes because without each of these you're just a victim, who just dwells in laziness, unclear about his or her own destinations.

The bottom line is that what you have is today, so rekindle the strings to best adaptively for a beautiful tomorrow. So, what's your strategy on working on your goals?

Sometimes, we destroy the beauty of the results by doubting our own abilities by making excuses. Believe in yourself; that is the first step toward s success.

Keep smiling – A living series

43
Walk Beyond

Wednesday, the 18th of February, and I just wonder where January vanished. Time runs away too fast and life is short. Afternoon is getting closer to set its way ahead, transforming into yet another pleasant day wrap and I find myself a little relaxed and in more peace today. Perhaps, not sure why and as if all is stopped for some time in the high rising concrete city of Mumbai and I find myself more inquisitive about what I'm doing with ideas which are moving like a roller coaster ride.

I decide to take up a book to read then reject the thought and pick up my phone to hear some music. Eventually, I decide to write as I am fascinated by the awesome sound of birds outside.

I might take some thirty minutes to write. Sitting in my room as I see a bright sunny day and chirping of birds that remind me the closest thing to experience the natural surroundings.

I stop to reflect in solitude with myself. Wondering at this moment while I'm busy writing, someone out may be smiling and someone may have lost someone close and may be mourning. I suddenly feel strange how the play is created in circles of smiles and tears.

Life is short like that of the golden shining dunes in the dessert which disappears on the arrivals of wind. Perhaps, like the clouds that gets transformed into rains as soon the winds arrive. So, I do now analyse that everything around is in the constant process of rebuilding or transformation into something new.

May I now correlate this sequence and refer the word as destinations. Does it sound like more statistical analysing the best way to get the truth out? Well, in that case, let me put it other way around.

Does the cloud need to die to get transformed into something new like rain? And if yes, what did the cloud achieve? Well, the answer is simple.

We have to understand the importance of life while inculcating the awareness of what is death. We need to struggle sometimes to grow into much better version of self. When life gets hard and things are not according to what we expect, let us not forget everyone experience this. Failures, hardships and hard times are common. Everyone goes through this route.

But, yes, during the gloomy times when nothing seems to be clear and everything appears to be blurring, keep paddling the cycle of life and remember that everything keeps on changing around us.

Seasons are never forecast for ever. Times change. Walk beyond to see what lies ahead. Hope beyond to explore what is stored in for you on the road ahead. Eventually, the clouds will disappear and the bright light of sun will shine. Sometimes, life keeps testing us and this can be a call for the change required.

God knows how far we can be tested and he would give us innumerable number of chances to recognise the opportunities ahead. If we just give up midway, thinking God has abandoned us, perhaps we are wrong. He would never let us walk alone during hard times.

And, yes, we need to believe in the light of faith; in the fire of hope; in God's will and wisdom.

We are given enough chances and enough of power to make best use of each new day to make the best paths towards our destinations. We are gifted with qualities and we should be obliged to share with others as we all need to understand to walk beyond the best of our own edges.

And dreaming about that we have plenty of time in future sound's pretty good but reality seems to be different sometimes. We have to listen to the inner voices sometimes and frame it as intuition.

No matter what life displays or however your current situation of life is- never underestimates the power of time. Everything is designed in the process of growth and change.

If we think rivers just flow or mountains just stand huge or trees just help us with shades and breeze. Just have a moment here to understand. Nothing is forever same.

Mountains are results of earthquakes. Just imagine how tremendously it must have been through the molten heat and lava finally adapted to the change accepting the challenge.

Finally, standing against all odds in all seasons facing rains, heat, winds, get eroded and get transformed into some different shape but doesn't lose its huge identity of giant structure, a standing symbol, a word for poets, a talk for inspires who write appraisals to lead the life strong and giant like that of mountains.

Thus, mountains pass the line to lead the life horizons as example and inspirations for many. And, perhaps, the silver line slates its good not to be same all time… keep transforming. Further expanding a little more on the life transformations, let me also refer the amazing transformations by a tree.

Though at one place it bears leaves fruits kept itself bare in winter and envelopes itself clothing's in the summers and again standing against all odds, facing all the changes of seasons, scattering seeds that start transforming into a new plant.

Despite being unaware of what lies ahead, we, the travellers to the life road should walk beyond our fears even if destinations are mysterious keep walking. And when we get there, we will be surprised and feel amazed to see back how far we travelled.

Walking beyond the lines of fears…

Keep smiling – A living series

44
Walk Like a Warrior

What's Positive Thinking? What's Being Positive? What's Being Courageous? All this just means Walk like a warrior towards the light. When there's a positive outlook for life there's no room for failures and there's no possibility of negatives around.

Positive Thinking;

Positive thinking may be defined as getting results for any situation in life by opting positive perception for all that's somehow viewed to be as complex and complicated.

But things may not be complicated or complex as perceived. Yes, negative perception plays all that can change everything. So, what's the best way to get the most outstanding results in the troubled situations of life?

When there's a positive outlook for life there's no place for being stressed. This develops the seeds of thinking good in all aspects of life and you slowly develop it as a habit and eventually become a positive thinker.

You no longer dwell in past and neither do you keep yourself occupied thinking of all those hundreds of things which may actually never happen.

Positive thinking never lets you lose choices that can change your life for better. Positive thinking leads your way towards more flourishing developments.

Instead of thinking what would go wrong, you can now choose what can be done now and you start exploring various other options to complete the task in hand and getting desired results. This leads to the path that sparks positive follows making you a successful visionary, who can now develop the status of finding peaceful solutions to all his problems.

This means being positive, you will now try and explore all the affirmative solutions in every situation of life. That's how a positive thinker would play his role. Indeed, amazing how thoughts, words, thinking may impact on the whole series of events in your life. This is needed to be understood and noted carefully.

Well, apart from this, positive thinking has a wider role to play and that can't be understood unless we view what's being positive.

Being positive;

At times, when you get fixed in darkest gloomy days when nothing seems to work out even though you try your best, just be a little patient. What's being positive? Well, as earlier said, being positive means nothing but thinking positive in every situation that you face.

Thinking positive or being positive is thinking for positive results or being more acceptable towards life in whatsoever life situations are by being balanced and keenly analysing in a more optimistic way.

When there's positive thinking or positive outlook, there's no room left for negatives to dwell and no space for negative assumptions.

Being positive ends up having a more pleasant life than someone who thinks only negative in every situation. Perhaps, they remain standing at the same place holding time, draining their energies with ultimate no progress in life missing every little opportunity that life must have forwarded towards them because those who look into negative things in life lack to see better options for the problems that they may be facing.

Sometimes, we just need to ignore the circumstances and move ahead with courage. Sometimes, ignoring is only the available solution. We got to keep ourselves engaged in other things so that we can avoid impacts of negatives. We usually get best answers to every question when we are in peace and in patience.

Being positive will not allow negative things or thoughts to invade the mind. This helps maintaining peace and results patience required to attain the best solutions or desired results of problematic situation.

Being positive helps you to look beyond your fears you tend to take risks.

Being positive helps you to adopt different ways towards sorting out the solutions for your problems.

Being positive helps you exploring different and wider approach towards achieving success in your task.

Being positive envelopes you in courage in a radiant attitude that helps you follow your dreams achieve your goals and leading you towards prosperity.

Positive thinking leads you to become being positive thus comprehending true courage that you can implement in your life and walk courageously like a warrior towards light.

Being Courageous;

When you opt being positive, you also encourage others who are fixed in negativity of life. Yes, it's not so easy but again it's not impossible either.

We can opt being positive and we can resonate positive energy around bringing about a drastic change in so many people around. Just think about this. Most people do accept positive energy spreading people.

Like you get a smile back to your smile, a blessing is followed by a blessing, likewise being positive is also contagious; just try with a little more courage. Change someone's gloomy day into light today. That's what I say, Being in courage. To take a risk overlooking negatives opting positives and spreading light.

There exist so many people who love to hear and feel good. Accept problems with a chance to challenge yourself and try to overcome the defeat by your positive perception today. Every morning brings innumerable number of chances to opt out for a change that you desire to see.

Rediscover this opportunity that life keeps adding day after day. Be privileged to be in this life. I personally like positive life brighter than anything else. And positive people do shine brighter.

And the benefits are endless. Positive thinking makes you a positive thinker.

Being a positive thinker you will be more courageous.

Being in courage often helps you to explore more success.

This overall evolves you a new person evading life with a powerful positive being. You now courageously open the doors of challenges which you escaped earlier. You now make your dreams come true.

You now achieve your goals

Being positive is a power that's undeniable, that's remarkable to have a great importance and can make impact on your life. Respect yourself to stand against fear every time you face it. Just be positive. Endeavour to learn a little more of patience and be optimistic in every situation that you face. Do not assume yourself as a victim of circumstances. Just hold your head high walk towards the light like a strong warrior.

Keep smiling – A living series

45

A Living Series Talk-Contrast and Hues

Contrast: The self-analysis

The most important and the hardest part of life is retrospections of our own self more precisely. Let me quote here self-awareness and self-analysis. We are more inclined to rationalize the things which we are not good at or we ignore to rectify our own flaws.

The change starts instantly when we ask ourselves every time we face an issue or are entangled in vulnerabilities. Thus, we do create a finest tool called awareness that helps us to de-clutter all our clogged thoughts. We have to constantly work upon our own weaknesses and work forward to walk ahead against what that tries to keep us holding back.

We have to improve ourselves on daily basis a little to come out of our current situations. We have to improvise and look beyond the frame sometimes. We have to analyse all the areas of disturbances around to understand why the things are not working. Yes, at times, the circumstances are unavoidable, but we can't give up in middle of the battle field. We have to keep fighting all the inner demons of weaknesses that form one of the major barriers between you and where you aim to reach. Now, try to research every little flaw, each and every string that is the reason and indirectly responsible. So, let it be even if it's your laziness. Do try to figure out in a most efficient way to get out of this web and infuse a little discipline and self-confidence. One of the other truths that most of the people are reluctant to hear about themselves is their own perceptions and the objectives that they carry to renovate the path that they laid for themselves as most of the important compounding factor is laziness. So, self-analyse and walk the path now.

Hues -The determination

The labour of hard work, skills and your performance, even at the uncertain times, and more evidently during the inevitable phase of those hard times that you've invested in life, is nothing but a concrete foundation, a tougher path that leads the way for your magnificent tomorrow. A tomorrow that still waits to embrace you and that would add a colour to all your unfulfilled dreams. Tile by tile, we cement our life into progress towards a more meaningful tomorrow that we weaved today so eloquently, so amicably, and explicitly.

A world of you, by you, and for you

We need to set some personal goals and induce some discipline in our daily routines and be prepared like a warrior for our journey to this beautiful life. An abundance of will power and strong determination can bring about fascinating performances. Try to constantly work on the improvements and do remember that if your approach is not filled in enthusiasm and flourished with positive thoughts, you are not reaching your goals in time. As the much needed fuels are being positive, self-belief and enthusiasm. And if there's any imbalance or any one of the element is missing somewhere, get started now and seek the missing links

Through the journey of -A Living Series, I intend to specify and express my poignant thoughts, my life experiences.

Yes, I see these lessons and experiences as an asset. If we do not work on time to replenish and refocus the life that we want, eventually we will be forced to live and spend our precious time dealing with a life that we do not desire to live. This is the right time to re-focus what you want from your life.

I intend to spark a hope an inspiration to all those, who are trying hard to come out the entangled adversities. I intend to show a little way out that I did learn through my struggling and hard times of life; my lessons learned through life experiences reflecting the best path chosen while times were still confusing and complex.

I believe strongly that being positive, believing in self- and thereby inculcating confidence within flowing with the key of faith and hope through life are triumph over sufferings and that the failures, hard times, difficult phases of life are just assets of experiences that come to make you what you deserve to be, making you brave enough to live your life of that what you dream. They are always crafting you, inhibiting the strength to focus and make you grow mentally, emotionally, and spiritually, thus enhancing the real personality that gets faded away during the despairs and devastating times thus sculpting you strong enough to view the things in more precision. And thus, conditioning you to keep checking as how far and tougher do you walk on the righteous path how efficiently you can keep balancing the things making our life worth living and searching the true path for what you believe.

Thus, now I wish my readers to get all the courage to manifest what you believe is right for you and all the courage to discover the real of you by discovering the need for a personal change.

Every step we have to accept the real challenges.

We can't live in illusions. We have to focus on and give our hundred percent doing justice to whatever we are doing no matter how much difficult or mundane it may appear we must make sure that we remain disciplined and determined.

Sufferings are nothing but a test, a test to check our resilience, a test of our compassion and thus fortifies our individual behaviour it is a first step towards change. Suffering is a test to check our weaknesses and our strength.

The best stories come from all the struggles we face on our way towards reaching our dreams. And the golden key or the gate pass is ***patience****. It is the ability to not react to the situations or circumstances but being calm, being relaxed at our nerves when we realize the reality check that disappointments, failures and troubles, delays in work or other projects, hardships are not a crack in the mould of life but a complete package of life that has to be faced boldly and with upmost honesty. When we accept this we improve our life exponentially thus making a fine tuning with the quality of the life we live.*

Some times are odd and very indecisive, but just believe in yourself. Remind yourself - "I can."

Keep smiling – A living series

Inderjit Kaur

Acknowledgements...

I am not perfect neither my life is flawless but I do believe in myself and that is the first step to make progress in our lives. And our life in nothing but work in progress with mixed events of some epic days and some days are filled with challenges. I did walk through dark valleys and pains and that is absolutely fine since that is life that keeps you going. And on this road I have been travelling I was fortunate to meet so many kind hearts whom I would like to acknowledge today.

A living series was not possible without the support of my family, my sons Mandeep and Arjun and friends who believed in me. I would like to thank everyone who walked and encouraged me time to time. I want to record the support and encouragement by Simarjit, Paul Hollis, Alpna Chhabra, Aparna Naidu, Renuka Nair, Joan Rocha and Vaidehi grateful to you always and also thankful to Effrosyni Moschoudi, Tamara Ferguson, Tamie Dearen, Carol Phipps, and Doug J Cooper for being my supportive Author friends.

This book would not have been complete without the Foreword presented by Award winning and Amazon best seller Author of "The Hollow Series" Paul Hollis. Thank you for encouraging me always and your continued kind support.

And finally, the loving divine energy that flows through my life every single day, I am grateful to ***Shirdi Sai*** for showing me the way to walk the right path of living

I want to also acknowledge my gratitude to Vandana Valsakumar for being so supportive at all the times also the entire publishing team and cover designer team at ***Notion Press*** and all the people who had a hand in making this possible.

About the Author

Inderjit Kaur is an author, motivator with a powerful voice of spreading positive words through her writings. A highly influential blogger and inspirational guide who with her tag line 'Keep smiling, keep shining,' has brewed up with the original concept of living through her books of

A living series

Inderjit Kaur a full time writer whose other books include-

Living a more meaningful life, Elements of life.

To receive a constant streaming of inspiration, follow Inderjit Kaur tweets and blogs following are the links…

@inderjitlmml

@Alivingseries

Link to Amazon Author page

http://www.amazon.com/-/e/B00TJHMCH4

Link to Good reads Author page

https://www.goodreads.com/inderjitkaur

Link to blog (A living series blog)

https://inderjitlmml.wordpress.com/

Link to blog (A living series talk)

https://alivingseriestalk.wordpress.com/

GLOSSARY

Zafarnama means the *"Declaration of Victory"* and is the name given to the letter sent by the tenth Sikh Guru, Guru Gobind Singh in 1705 to the Emperor of India, Aurangzeb. The letter is written in exquisite Persian verse. In this letter, Guru Ji reminds Aurangzeb how he and his henchmen had broken their oaths taken on the holy Koran.

Despite this deception, this treacherous leader could not harm the Guru. Guru Ji states in this letter that in spite of his several sufferings, he had won a moral victory over the crafty Mughal who had broken all his vows and had resorted to underhand behaviour. Despite sending a huge army to capture or kill the Guru, the Mughal forces did not succeed in their mission.

Bichitra Natak (or Bachittar/Vichitra) (meaning Resplendent Drama) is a beautiful composition, a memoir of Guru Gobind Singh (Tenth Guru Sikh) which he added in Dasam Granth, commonly known as his Brief Autobiography. It is a part of the Dasm Granth holy scriptures of the Sikhs This text spans from page 94 to page 175 of the 2326 pages of this holy book of the Sikhs (Original text is over 1428 pages)

This is an autobiographical narrated by the tenth Guru Gobind Singh for the first 32 years of his life. Although the word "Natak" means "drama" in Punjabi, this is no drama though. The Guru has outlined the circumstance and history of the time and how great courage and strength was required to overcome the many hurdles that were upon the community.

It starts with a praise of God It then gives a genealogy of Bedis and Sodhis also gives the author's own biography and includes the description of various during Mughal Era in Punjab. Up to AD 1696.

The Dasam Granth: historically known as Dasven Padshah Ka Granth(Punjabi: Book of the Tenth Emperor) is a Scripture of Sikhism of containing texts composed by the 10th Sikh Guru Gobind Singh. The compositions of the Granth set out the ideas, thoughts and guidelines for the future of the Nanak panth as enshrined in the Khalsa. The Jaap Sahib, Tvye Prasad Sawaiye (Amrit Savaiye) and Benti Chaupai are all compositions from the Dasam Granth, are part of the daily prayers of the Sikhs which serve, as well, as a part of the Sikh initiation. The beginning portion of the daily Ardaas for Sikhs is also a composition within the Dasam Granth.